LIBRARIES UNLIMITED
Please return/renew this ite
Renew on tel 0345 1...

As the following is a true story, all characters in this book
are real – you know who you are.
If you happen to resemble these persons, it's an absolute coincidence.
For privacy, surnames have been omitted.

Text and illustrations copyright Amy Whitewick, 2015.

All rights reserved. No part of this publication may be reproduced, stored in a retrieval system, or transmitted in any form by means, electronic, mechanical, photocopying, recording or otherwise, without prior permission of the author.

www.camelotmedia.co.uk

Printed by CreateSpace

Featured in:

The No.1 free waterways newspaper

AN AMUSING JOURNAL FROM AMY WHITEWICK

from the author

The canal is perhaps the most humorous place I know of in Britain, owing to awkward living conditions, the close proximity of well-stocked pubs and the presence of persons from all walks of life. Every time I step onto the towpath there is something to muse about, especially when the brain can celebrate its freedom and wander off its lead to pee up the nearest mooring pin.

Originally, I used to have a narrowboat – and a jolly nice one it was too. Fortunately, as a family, Mum, Dad and I learned the hard introductory lessons from her a while ago and had a whale of a time over five years cruising up and down the Kennet and Avon revelling with exciting new friends. After that we had to wave 'bye bye' to her, what with demanding jobs and life 'things'.

A couple of years later we found ourselves falling in love with a fat boat. Wide beams are the bane of every narrowboater's life, and yes, even we used to cringe when seeing one coming in the opposite direction. It was like seeing a cargo ship coming at a canoe. Now we see life on the other side, and if people tell you the grass is greener, it most certainly is and you should absolutely believe them. Big is best.

If I were to boast I would tell you we now have enough space to park two cars side by side indoors (minis, maybe), two bedrooms (no more make-up beds and odd sharing arrangements) and a BATH.

Sadly, as we all know, buying a second-hand boat is never plain sailing, and engine/bathroom/electric/plumbing issues always pop out of the woodwork like those scary beetles that live in churches.

Although rather dull problems to have, I hope the following renders a slightly more comical side to how we tackled learning the ropes on our new girl. Perhaps, it too, will shine a light on your own girl out there, or someone else's, and show that there is indeed, a funny side to every situation (after a few glasses of wine).

I must, however warn that the following journal, although true to life and expressed in great detail is indeed, full of sh*t, quite literally. Toilet humour features a great deal, and although I don't often share it in social situations, these pages offer the perfect opportunity to express a more creative side to boating. I do apologise if you are unaccustomed to words such as 'cleavage' and 'turds'. These words are equally balanced with the quintessential British word 'marvellous', but I can assure you that they do not reside in the same sentence.

The characters in this book are real people, and if you're one of them, firstly, I apologise, secondly, well done you're famous, thirdly, you're all fantastic friends and I appreciate your actions, however small, that have helped inspire and write this journal, that I know many will grin at, and others will tease you over or talk about during a tea ritual.

One of my pet hates is seeing books and magazines in the bathroom, next to the toilet. I dearly hope the following doesn't end up there, and if it does – well, I'm sure the ink on the pages will leave a lasting impression somewhere.

If it's in a bathroom on a boat, I sympathise with you – it's difficult enough to find room for a box of cereals, let alone a book.

Some of the entries to follow you may well recognise from editions of the Towpath Talk. The Editor has been very kind to allow me to reshare them (a modern social networking term) for your enjoyment – I hope you enjoy this journey as much as we did on our Fat Boat.

Before you read on...

To be as true-to-life as possible, I have represented the journal in order of the time it was written – Towpath Talk specials are planned ahead of schedule, so hence appear to lurk amongst earlier months.

9th August
We bought a fat boat

Today we bought a fat boat.

Yes, the great, tank-like bath tubs we used to sneer at on the canal. You know the ones – they cloggle up the canal, greedily keeping locks to themselves and their owners sit smarmily out on deck chairs on an enlarged bow.

We actually bought one. And we love it – well, her, to be polite and correct.

We exchanged on the bow today with one of her lovely owners, who, with a smile (and a rather hard bump of his head on the doorway) shook hands and took his belongings and his smoking pipe away with him, a tear in his eye. He looked back one last time at her, and I remembered that look and feeling when we sold our narrowboat three years ago to become land huggers once more. Now we've got a fat boat – double the pleasure, and double the work, challenge accepted.

It all happened within a matter of days – Dad went to the marina to enquire about a mooring in case we decided to buy a boat, and there, lo and behold, was our fat boat, barely seconds in her mooring and about to go to the brokers.

Today we sat, still reeling slightly from the shock, sipping champagne whilst exploring our new best friend. Pulling back the sofa revealed two tennis balls, plus, to my excitement, a miniature

Narnia-like cupboard tucked deep behind it out of sight, with nothing more interesting than the gas valve for the cooker inside. Still, it was worth a try.

We can't get over the masses of space compared to our old narrowboat, who, bless her, was indeed a great deal skinnier and had trouble keeping still. To be honest, so did we, trying to dance around each other in a 1ft wide corridor. Cooking a breakfast used to be interesting to say the least.

Now, we waft around looking excitedly inside every cupboard and drawer, lifting up mattresses (don't ask), pressing switches and inspecting mushrooms. Not the magic ones, but the ones that live on the roof – the brass ones, of course.

The television is, after all, the most important feature, and after discovering we can in fact get ITV 1, we breathed a sigh of relief, knowing that as long as we are in the marina by 7pm, we will always get Emmerdale. Goodness knows what will happen if we go out on the towpath at that time of day, perhaps the world will end. Or the recording button will save us, whichever comes first.

Amazingly, we have something affectionately called 'the shed' at the back end of the boat, so called because of the many shelves lined in peculiar cans and baskets of hammers, wire, a spirit level and other items that any man would be proud of to have in his cave.

To top it all off, there's the fancy gauge for the solar panels (awesome) and the engine below, which I haven't been brave enough to look at yet, hence a visit is due shortly from our South African engineering friend, Ron, who is very fierce with a spanner. Goodness knows what will happen if he encounters our other South African friend, Iain, who can scare the pants off of anybody (except us, of course).

They tell you to keep your friends close – they're handy, that's why. You only keep your enemies closer so you can keep an eye on them and make sure they're not stealing your shoreline electric when you have your back turned.

After exploring the bathroom and discovering that at very least we had half a toilet roll kindly left for us, I found something that made my face light up like a Christmas tree. A tank waste gauge. With a little red needle. And – you'll never guess – it actually TELLS you when your poo tank is full!

You might wonder why I'm so excited, but all our narrowboat had was a little red light that lit up near the time. With absolutely no inkling what so ever (I like at least a week's notice) we would constantly gaze at the red light thinking, is it full now? Do we need to immediately pump out, or do we play the waiting game? Thankfully, we never got the chance to find out what happens when it's totally full and you flush.

Another pants-wetting moment – we have a bath, an actual BATH. We don't even have one of those at home and I can't remember the last time I saw one (except at a posh B and B, where it had legs on it). This one doesn't have legs, but it does resemble a bath, which is a great bonus.

I did get told off for pulling a bit of carpet off the wall. Yes, not the floor, the wall. To keep it warm in winter. You can't blame me, it's something called curiosity, and I was only testing the glue. And seeing if I could pull it off in the same manner as a wine bottle label (I'm dangerous at parties – wine swap, anyone?).

Dad got into trouble for pulling off the internal mushroom vent. Bits of things came down into Mum's wine glass – champagne does not require seasoning, especially with boat fluff.

A duck looked at us through the window with a 'are you mad?' expression, and I did wonder for a minute, then shook my head.

'No, it's the most exciting project we've ever taken on.'

I glanced at the bowl of oranges left on the shelf below the television, their bright glow the only splash of colour in the boat.

'And, perhaps, the strangest.'

10th August
Sticks like Sh*t

We went to a friend's surprise 65th birthday party today, a long way from the canal. Our mind, however, was still reeling with excitement of our new girl. It was a job to contain ourselves when someone asked if the canal was near us. Then came the question: 'do you have a barge?'

I almost combusted with the indecision of whether or not I, or any of us should tell them. Instead of a wise and eloquent phrase such as 'oh, yes indeed we do, a 55ft by 12ft one, it just recently came into our possession.', a feeble, 'ermmm, yes, um, sort of...' Escaped my lips.

The tricky subject was quickly changed as dinner arrived in the form of a hog roast and our attentions turned to keeping the marquee tied down whilst balancing a plate of food – no mean feat in 40mph gusts of wind kindly given to us by the remnants of hurricane Bertha.

There was one advantage I discovered today – sit downwind of someone else who is eating and receive seconds on your plate without needing to leave your seat. There is a downside to this, however, when it comes to the chocolate fudge cake pudding which sticks like shit to crockery and refuses to budge, even with 60mph blast.

A jet wash is required for these sorts of occasions.

Earlier this morning we did stop over to check the boat after last night's heavy rains – so far she seems dry – the engine bay may yet need a pantyliner to control the small damp puddles produced by the pounding rain dribbling under her hatch.

Still excited over the dramatic increase in space which we explored once more, we left wet patches of our own after realising we didn't have any doormats (you need two on a boat, one at each end).

They're not only great for controlling feet-shaped puddles, but also other oddities which may try to sneak on board undetected on the underside of your shoe.

Curious, I had a brief rummage in the shed and found a large china mug with 'first class Dad' written on it (guess who that now belongs to) amongst other strange items, including a t-bar shaped key which I have absolutely no idea where it belongs. The other t-bar shaped key is for the pump out tank, but this one looks like it's important, mounted on its own special little bracket. I'm sure we'll find a use for it.

I still can't believe we have a boat with a proper sofa on. Wow.

12th August
Don't ask me

We've been visiting the boat in small doses over the past few days and yet, she feels like a drug. I have a hard time not thinking about her, and when I do, I drift off into a world of my own, and people look at me, slightly concerned, nudging me to see if I'm still there.

Some of the best excuses to come from my mouth so far have been: 'Oh, sorry, I got distracted as I'm so hungry', or 'Wow, is that a chocolate gateau?' Or the best one, 'Sorry, I was thinking about a roast dinner after that logo I designed recently for a catering van, it looks good enough to eat.'

Always blame it on food – it's a common obsession and people don't think you've completely lost it. Well, not yet, anyway (most people think I already have, so it doesn't make much difference).

Today we went for a surprise birthday party for one of my customers whose business is barely a couple of feet from the marina where the boat is kept, and for the first time, we actually told someone we had bought a boat. It was a bizarre feeling, and we were still only getting used to the idea at the time, but by the evening it felt real again.

We went to our girl after a stressful day dealing with work problems. The marina in comparison was rewardingly quiet and gentle, the water rippling in the breeze and ducks bobbing on the miniature waves.

I sat for a while on the shed floor, watching Dad nimbly wiring a shoreline cable plug together, whilst I stared in awe.

I have no idea how to wire anything and failed at soldering circuit boards at school, hence my concentration wandered and I went rummaging through the shelves and inspecting the contents of a yellow basket left for us with a dozen other plugs scattered inside (don't ask me how to wire them).

Soon enough, we had a working shoreline cable and rejoiced in the fact we have a choice of two exterior sockets, as technically we have two mooring spaces, being a fat boat. Sockets 161 and 162 are ours to select at random – life is all about variety.

I have been curious to know what would happen if we were to switch with one of our neighbours and whether they would notice if we use their electric for a while to do a spot of hoovering, or put the toaster on at the same time as the kettle. The trouble is, I have a conscience and it doesn't let me do things like that. It doesn't want me to be on Santa's naughty list either.

We checked the boat over once more and Dad sat in the recently cleaned leather armchair with a 'poof!' We reflected on how pleasant people are on the canal compared to living on land. Everyone seems happy and smiley on the canal – even couples walk together in full sight of everyone without peering round corners to check if anyone is watching in public.

It seems to me, everyone on the canal is on the same level, or, excuse the pun, 'in the same boat'. It doesn't matter who you are, whether you have money or not – it's your personality and your skills that matter. People take you for how you appear in that moment, and our experience of the canal shows you can be in any predicament and people will help you (our narrowboat flooded once from a burst shower pipe and the kind boaters moored in front of us came to a rescue with an aqua vac to save us hours of bucket-bailing in the freezing cold).

If only land people were the same. My experiences of them are often very poor ones.

Thankfully, I'm no longer one of them.

14th August
Hidden Surprises

It was Dad's turn today to go to the boat after picking up African Ron who came with his fierce set of spanners to inspect our girl from top to bottom, his nimble fingers searching her engine and advising us what the grease lever was. Apparently lots of boats have them and it was totally normal. Good job you don't have to give a couple of turns to one before you start and finish your car journey, or you'd be in the service station two hours spending a fortune on doughnuts whilst waiting for the engine to cool down.

Thankfully African Ron discovered a few hidden surprises including some scorched live wires that were touching the engine (we were lucky the boat didn't burst into flames) and some water under the floor of the boat which has built up out of condensation etc over the years and left a small pool a few goldfish would be delighted with.

We've been told we need an aqua vac, the sofa moved to the other side of the boat to tilt it a bit and several elephants to stand on the gunnels for us. Apparently the elephants are to help with tilting the boat and getting the water to drain to the hatch where the water hoover will go to suck it away.

African Ron was delighted when Mum popped up with a beer and a brolly for him, to keep him both wet and dry at the same time. Marvellous what beer can do.

After placing back the labyrinth of panels to cover up our girl's modesty (her private engine bits) Dad took African Ron home and

Mum went to get some rather fetching tester pots for the interior paint. Amusingly they have ridiculous names (as all paint does) including 'Acorn', 'Kitchen green' and 'Pea green'.

There's certainly nothing green in my kitchen except vegetables and the odd bit of Stilton. We're going to try them out by painting teeny squares on the walls on Saturday and stare at them for half a day to work out which one would best suit our tastes. Knowing Dad, he'll pick 'British racing green' whilst Mum and I stare at each other in horror.

We're hoping for a maiden voyage on our girl to Sells Green and back on Saturday, with a brief stop at the pub for some lunch and some careful steering back into the marina to moor up once more.

I can't wait to stay on her next year when our work is complete and, whilst lying in bed, we hear the owls in the night beside the towpath and the birdsong early in the morning coming through the mushroom vents – it's truly magical.

16th August
Maiden Voyage

Today was our maiden voyage – although it's supposed to be summer, the weather is refusing to be fair game and blessed us with 40mph winds. Which is of course, marvellous for boating in. On the sea with a sailing ship perhaps.

Before setting off, Mum sucked the sofa to death with the hoover (I'm surprised there's anything left of it) and painted two swatches of green on the walls which matched our neighbour's boat perfectly, so that if we have the blinds open we wouldn't know where the wall ends and the window begins. The 'Pea green' didn't make the swatch stage as it looked slightly too violent, a shade resembling something that might crawl out of the pot by itself.

Even the bowl of oranges cringed at the thought and wrinkled in disgust.

After fumbling with a half-mile pile of ropes like a bunch of novices, we started the engine and were off, the wind blowing us out of the mooring a treat. In fact, too much of a treat, causing our other neighbours to look around nervously, watching as we guided our girl around their bows, smiling sweetly as we passed.

We passed the initiation test by getting out of the narrow marina entrance with barely a few centimetres to spare and glided along beside the boats moored on the towpath, and lo and behold, we passed our old narrowboat, still well cared for and loved by her new owners.

We smiled fondly as we passed her, patting our new girl gently, cooing, 'that's our old boaty over there. You're ours now.' People on the towpath probably thought we were crazy,

A few of them commented on the size of our new girl. 'Gosh, isn't it wide! 12ft – that's huge!' It's a good job she isn't human, or that would end up a serious insult, probably resulting in a punch up.

We discovered a wonderful aspect of owning a wide beam today. Everyone else moves out of the way. No more stopping, holding back. It seems narrowboats want absolutely nothing to do with a tank like ours and refuse to go anywhere near it, fear taking their faces into whole new territories of contorted terror as we approach.

Bridges with blind exits are enormous fun and Dad delighted in blowing the acoustic canned air horn (another goody left by our girl's previous owners) at every opportunity, letting every approaching boat within earshot know that something huge is coming their way and will result in a quick dash into the shrubbery and a panic attack on their part. How times have changed since owning a narrowboat.

We were lucky today and didn't need to jump off to do the swing bridge as a lady kindly waited for us, having no idea that we were about to go through, turn around and come back. When I opened my mouth to say so, she said she would shut the bridge whilst we turned and leave us as she was in a hurry. When Dad said something to her from the back of the boat she decided to wait. What a misery. Perhaps I approached her wrong with a smile as I told her what we intended to do. She looked the type that if she smiled back she might combust with the effort.

Sitting on the bow of the boat (or driving) is like being a celebrity. Everyone on the towpath waves, smiles, says good morning, good afternoon or whatever it is to you. I've since improved my hand wave to one similar to the queen which works excellent. You just sit there and people who are miserable just can't help themselves and HAVE to look up at you and grunt. I just have to perfect the art of people throwing money at the magic waving money box and that should just about buy us a new set of kitchen units after one weekend, judging by the towpath footfall.

On the way to our stop point, we checked the engine hatch whilst our girl was chugging along to see what was stirring beneath. The excitement was just too much for her, and she wet herself prolifically into the bilge, causing slight concern and constant gazing at the bilge bucket and non-functional pump which was about as much use as a chocolate fire guard.

I picked up a nasty habit of slamming the engine hatch and nearly burst and eardrum doing so. Next time I'll shut her quietly, lesson learned.

We stopped at our mooring to have lunch at our favourite general pub, the Three Magpies, munching our way through two courses. The pudding was great, but the pancake stack was more of a slide and didn't have enough pancakes. To me, a stack is at least six inches.

All the same, we stopped for a rest on the bow of the boat to feed some greedy ducks and got investigated by a group of swans who tried to nibble my arm. Very cute.

We left the visitor moorings refreshed and happy, congratulated by a fellow boater on our 'appropriate speed' – 'jolly good, well done, so nice to see someone go by slowly' – not like the hire boaters who passed us and him and at top speed a few minutes before, leaving Mum's sea legs well and truly behind.

As we made it back to the marina, I had the opportunity to drive and delighted in watching the swallows dart and dive around the boat, almost touching the front of it where Mum and Dad stood.

The wind picked up to a howling gale through the marina entrance and Dad had a job to squeeze through, as we were blown back out like a piece of paper.

A good rev from our girl and she was in once more, chugging around to our mooring. A couple of terns (birds that look like a bizarre cross between a swallow and a seagull) hunkered down on the jetties nearby, screeching and taking to the air as we passed.

With a sigh of relief, we made it back into our mooring and tied her up gently after her hard work, coiling the spare rope like a snake charmer's basket on the front (presentation is everything) and sank down into the sofa indoors, picking giant thistle seeds off of everything as they blew into the boat. Soon, we'll have them growing inside with the amount of dirt on the floor.

We discovered the wet nappy issue earlier in the engine bay was due to this strange grease tap we have to screw down every time we move the boat. Apparently she wasn't sealed enough, hence we have to constipate her every time we even think of going anywhere.

We tucked her up for bed and left her happy, snug as a bug next to our neighbours as we drove away, looking back at her fondly. 'Till next time.

17th August
Never Hand a Lady a Bag of Spanners

So much for summer. This morning bought thick drizzle and irritating gales which blew the miserable mist into every nook and cranny from your pants down to your socks. Now and then the weather would pause, leading you down the garden path in terms of being hopeful that it might stop. Only the ducks and geese at the marina appeared overjoyed at the prospect of even more water falling from the sky.

We clambered onto the boat and Dad fiddled with the knobs on the radiators – now I know what the teeny key in the kitchen drawer was for – the knife left in there I'm slightly concerned about. Perhaps it was to keep the monsters that gurgle in the heating system at bay.

The heating itself started up like that of a jet engine, leaving us clamping our ears and freezing to the spot as the noise grew to a higher pitch. I had serious considerations of jumping out of the swan hatch as it got higher, but found my feet glued firmly to the floor in anticipation of an explosion.

Either Dad couldn't hear it, or he pretended he couldn't, as he wandered around feeling the radiators and explaining things about plumbing that were way beyond my knowledge. All I know is you press a button and magically the monster in the engine bay uncurls itself, roaring and burbling and, just like magic, there's something called heating. On a boat.

After getting over the excitement of some warmth, it was time to get down and dirty with our girl down in the pits. I only thought there was one pit, but there seems to be three. Or maybe four, I lost count whilst figuring out the combination to replace the boards by.

Dad climbed into pit one and I sat and watched him as he pointed and pulled things out of her naughty parts and checked dipsticks and other strange orifices. I discovered a whole new world down below (it was like journey to the centre of the earth) with chasms of rust patches, a miniature sea in the bilge bucket and a monstrous-sized spider that crawled up the pipe work to stare at Dad. It was so big, I'm surprised Dad didn't shake its hand.

In pit two (in the shed) came another couple of naughty bits including a dipstick for oil and a water hole (not the sort you get in Africa with rhinos and zebras crowded around). A quick skinny dip of the fingers made sure our girl was well-hydrated. Her green engine body is marvellously shiny, so much so, I am terrified of putting a dirty foot mark on it. It actually made the spanners look dull next to it.

I passed Dad a few after rummaging in the bottomless bag he bought along from home which has about fifty different sizes in.

'Hand me a spanner.'

All well and good.

'Which one?'.

You always end up with the one that doesn't quite fit, so you have to rummage again to find the next size down or up. Never hand a lady a bag full of spanners. It's very dangerous in the wrong hands.

I used to consider owning a horse. Now I have fifty of them! Well, sort of. Apparently the engine is 50 horsepower – a big step up from our measly 35hp on our old narrowboat. In the good old days 50 horsepower pulling a boat with ropes meant you had to seriously consider getting out of the way or end up a flattened pancake in the dust. Nowadays it's only the cyclists on the towpath that actively seek to mow you down at any given opportunity.

After finishing playing with spanners and grease, we retreated into the boat, marvelling at the new-found kitchen space where the fridge and microwave had been. Yesterday morning was a real treat and both were disposed of at the local dump, polar bears and all.

The ice somehow remained intact and refused to melt, much to Dad's disgust, as he expected to have a chuckle by driving along in the truck with the meltwater spewing along behind and decorating the windscreen of prospect tailgaters. Instead, the polar bears wandered off in search of the nearest champagne bucket to cool off in and celebrate their release into the wild.

This morning Dad decided to tackle cleaning the back of the sofa (an excellent effort achieved in just five minutes, a record time for a surface area bigger than our dining room table at home).

He handed me a bucket to take back to the shed whilst he nipped to the loo. Casually, I took my time in the shed, admiring the scenery from the back doors of rolling distant hills swathed in fluffy cloud.

As I breathed in deep, the toilet flushed. And I forgot. There's a toilet tank vent at the back of the boat.

The smell was horrific, so much so, I had to check the contents of the bucket, just to make sure there wasn't something lurking in there by mistake. In one quick bound, I dropped the bucket and dashed down inside the boat back to the kitchen, face next to the window for a gulp of fresh air, staring at Dad as he came out of the loo.

He frowned.

'What's the matter with you?'

I looked at him again.

'Nothing. By the way, that smell – it wasn't me.'

I haven't used the toilet yet. I'm worried that if I do, something might get stuck and the macerator teeth might growl at me and refuse to dispose of something unmentionable.

How embarrassing.

18th August
Pink Boats

Our license arrived today – hoorah! And, amazingly, the canal and River Trust have matched this year's display paper colour to the soon-to-be painted green interior.

Either they've been spying on us or it's just a coincidence, I'm not so sure. I reckon we should all have a chance to vote on next year's colour.

Pink would be a real hoot and ensure even more boaters didn't pay their license for fear of people getting the wrong impression from the towpath. Orange would be nice and clash with the traditional red, perhaps persuading boaters to be a bit more brave with their colour schemes.

I did see a whole pink narrowboat once. It was horrifying, like a life-sized version of a Barbie play set, but with Ken driving whilst Barbie played in the bath inside. It gives me the shudders every time I think of it.

As it was a work day, I did have to plough through the 'w' word for most of the day, but was let off the leash for a few hours to see some of our marvellous friends who we used to edit the Kennet and Avon Canal trust's magazine, the Butty, with.

Together we wined and dined at the Barge Inn, Honeystreet. Whilst waiting for them, we took a moment to wander the towpath past a few moored boats and reflected on how quiet it was.

At home, all you can hear on a windy day is the main road, and on the towpath, cyclists roar by and groups of people like packs of bouncers squeeze past you, treading in the odd dog turd or two as they do so. This towpath looked very clean.

On the way into the pub we saw one of our boating friends who shook our hands, smiling his broad grin and patting Dad on the back. He called me 'babes'.

I'm not sure quite what to make of that term yet, but I grinned back anyway, eyes darting quickly to the cider pumps. I chose a risky looking one labelled 'Area 51'.

Perhaps that's where you end up after drinking a couple of pints of it, who knows. I stuck with a half, just in case it had any funny ideas on reprogramming my legs.

We picked the biggest table in the pub and sat laughing and chatting our way through our meals. Mike ended up with a huge spider on his glasses, and after a frightened flick, it landed perfectly on Dad's jumper, earning a gold medal in the gymnastic category at the same time. It soon ended up a snack for the pub cat, which obviously looked hungry after pacing up and down the table several times (I did take pleasure in throwing it off once).

It was marvellous to talk canal with our friends who actually understand the challenges of boating and the relaxation it can bring to those such as us who choose not to holiday abroad each year and prefer the comfort of our own homes. And boats, of course.

I went out tonight with my friend's horses (he taught me how to carriage drive them), and whilst tugging them gently round a corner, a thought popped into my head.

How is horsepower measured?

At that moment, one of the horses let rip an enormous fart, temporarily popping the bubble in which the question appeared.

Later on, I remembered again and Googled it, discovering that one horsepower is equivalent to the power required to lift 33,000 pounds one foot in one minute.

We have 50 horsepower in our girl's engine, and as of yet, it hasn't been able to lift the boat barely an inch out of the water, but it does do a wonderful job propelling it forwards. A floating object is a bit different to a static weight, so does horsepower change in water? Old narrowboats were one horsepower, equivalent to one horse, one rope pulling one boat over several hours. Big difference there.

Another bizarre question that popped into my head today was, what happens when, say for instance, a duck goes to the toilet in water? Does it have a safety valve, or does the duck sink out of sight like the Loch Ness monster, hence why you never see a duck do a dump when swimming? I haven't, anyway.

Mum suggested perhaps it has its own grease tap and requires packing (or pecking as ducks call it) to fill the gap. Who knows – I'm not Googling that one.

20th August
An Obsession

I haven't seen the boat for a couple of days now (some of us who own boats do work, you know), hence the withdrawal symptoms growing stronger than ever.

We ran out of cider and wine tonight, and that made matters even worse. I could tell by Mum's slip of the tongue that things were getting desperate when she described a pair of rubber gloves as welly gloves. They might as well be.

Dad, however, did get the chance to go today and took Andrew with him, a nice man who fitted out our previous boat, and does a wonderful job with a saw and a slice of sandpaper.

Apparently, he thought the boat is marvellous, and measured up for our new set of front steps that lead down in from the bow. He did a fantastic job at home building a set of stairs that we use every day and they're still there after seven years, so we can at least trust him. His latest ventures have included making giant wooden camels – as long as he doesn't build our steps with a couple of Bactrian-sized humps in, we'll be fine.

Our girl is due another visit on Sunday by a man called Dave who is going to look at her over-active bladder problem. She still seems to drip a little too much for our liking (nighttime pull-ups do NOT work on boats) and the pump still isn't working. I'm sure she's doing this on purpose, just to get all these charming men on board fondling her bits and bobs. Naughty thing.

Just as a new home requires furniture, as does a boat, so we went off around B&Q and Wickes this evening to nosy around their kitchen displays, 'oohing', 'aahing', stroking surfaces and looking puzzled at drawers with no handles. Apparently, this is the in thing. Our eyes caught a nice unit with a rounded end and we touched it fondly. Dad and I quickly found the most important item of furniture – the wine rack. We told Mum there's no need to buy any other units, the wine rack will do just fine. That, and a fridge – to keep it cold before drinking, of course.

The taps were another issue all together – some were stupendously ugly (goodness knows who designed them) and others were out-of-this-world enormous and large enough to hang a bath towel on whilst you washed.

All we wanted was a simple bathroom tap. They're not called taps on the labels. They're called 'basin mixers'. It probably means they play awesome tunes with dramatic basal tones perfect for the echoing bathroom environment. Or something like that. Either way, we'll find out soon enough.

As we wandered back through the kitchen section, I spotted a row of toilet seats and crowed in delight (I do have an excellent taste in toilet humour), and shouted very loudly whilst pointing at one which resembled a fish tank.

A couple sat talking to the kitchen salesman in his little open plan office stared as if I were some lunatic that had never seen a toilet seat before. It's not every day you have so much choice. They were certainly much cheaper than the one Dad had to order for our boat loo (there's no way I'm perching on the one that's there now).

He ordered it yesterday outside, whilst we read through the frightening paperwork that stated never to EVER flush if there's something you haven't eaten first (I never get this, as you technically don't eat your turds first, unless you're a rabbit, then you do it several times).

A wasp at that moment of reading tried to attack us and had no chance, being hit in the face by a picture of a saniflow toilet. Good job it wasn't a real toilet – then the wasp would have felt it as well as seen it (and probably smelled it, too).

Back in B&Q, we rushed around, grabbing rolls of lining paper, wallpaper paste and brushes, in which I took great delight in stroking each one, carefully rolled in their own little wrappers like little hairy mice. Dad chose the quality ones which felt like touching a guinea pig that recently used hair conditioner. If that doesn't leave a smooth finish, perhaps some anti-frizz cream will do the trick.

Exhausted, we walked out of the shop looking like a trio of decorators, tubs swinging from our arms and paper rolls under our arms.

After tucking it all into the boot, Dad went off into Halfords next door to look for some anti-freeze, but couldn't find the right one.

There's so many different types, it's a job to choose. It's like trying to pick a juice drink – ready mixed, concentrated, blah, blah, blah, don't drink, dangerous for the environment, produced in a factory that handles nuts – no, wait, that's just juice.

Bored with reading bottles, I looked around. I have never seen so many wiper blades for sale, enough to line up end-to-end to cross the English Channel. It's just not normal.

Whilst I gawped at them, I wondered why my brother wasn't in here, owing to his obsession with anything that has a wheel in each corner. Then I realised. There's more than one Halfords. And I can't talk. I have an obsession with a fat boat.

24th August
Why Didn't We Think of That?

As usual, August Bank holiday always means one thing – RAIN.

Actually, we've been very fortunate the past few days in that it has been very dry. Until this morning, that is. The plan was to paint the boat roof early this morning, until we discovered Mother Nature had left a lovely gift of a thick blanket of dew to keep the boat cosy, and make Dad frustrated.

Watered down paint is not a good idea, hence the rush to grab everything that could absorb water out of the boat and spread it across the roof.

We went through about four jey clothes, twenty sheets of kitchen roll and a lot of puffing and grunting until Dad spotted a neighbour standing on the roof of his boat casually sweeping water off the top with a broom. We stared at each other, mouths agog. Why on earth didn't we think of that?

After another half an hour of sweeping, mopping and sponging, the roof didn't look any drier, and Dad's trousers were in an even worse state than the roof.

Whilst he went home to change, I sat and finished polishing the tiller (which looked as though it had never seen a tin of Brasso in its life) until it sparkled like gold.

Our neighbours probably thought I was slightly insane, lovingly stroking it up and down and twirling it in the sun. They should be envious. It's a total embarrassment to go out with a tiller that you can't at least see your face in (or anyone else's for that matter).

Now it serves as a spare mirror in the shed (great for checking salad in your teeth, or that kind of thing).

Dad came back a while later, and, when the roof finally started to dry, Dad whipped out the roller and painted it.

When I looked up a couple of hours later after polishing an awkwardly-shaped tiller pin, I had to shield my eyes.

The colour is fab, a lovely Cornish cream colour – but the shininess, well. If no one moved out of the way on the cut before, they will now, partially out of fear of the twelve-foot wide tank moving towards them with nowhere to go, and the other half out of blindness from the dazzling sunlight reflecting off of our girl's striking roof. Move over blonde bombshell, cream is the colour, baby, yeah.

Even the marina manager approved when he popped over for a quick chat. He's a remarkable man, easily recognised by his luminous blue braces and fast walk, with an air of your head teacher at school. You have to be on your best behaviour whenever he looks in your direction – it is his and his wife's marina to manage, after all.

And a great job they do of it too (I'm not just saying that because he's looking over here through his binoculars whilst I write this).

Mum joined us at lunch for, yep, you guessed it, lunch, after breaking into the brand new toaster left for us by the boat's previous owners.

It does about two slices at a time in its monstrously ugly white box thing, barely touching the sides with no hint of brown – but it still resembled toast when bitten in to.

Tea came shortly, and we indulged in our first meal on our girl, balancing the plates on our lap. The table is yet to come, a lesser commodity compared with other necessaries such as a toilet seat, something that we have to buy again, as the one we ordered online does not fit. The toilet that is, not our arses – just what size did you think we were? The wasp we hit with the paperwork is now smirking itself silly.

Engineer Dave turned up as planned this afternoon with a big grin and a box of bits.

I opened the bilge hatch for him, and down he went into Wonderland below, quick as a rabbit. It was only when he was down there did I tell him about the enormous spiders (the ultimate test of a proper man). He shuddered briefly, but carried on.

Our girl approved by making sure he was hit on the head a few times by the hatch. Such a naughty tease.

Dave fiddled with her loose bits, pulling up her boards to inspect the wiring beneath with a tut. 'Deary me, look, your engine buzzer is only held on by a piece of tape. Do you know what this is?' He pointed and I looked hurriedly round for Dad, out of my depth.

'Erm, not really, no, but I know they've put the engine reader the wrong way round', pointing in a totally different direction and changing the subject. I call it the engine reader, but really it's a display which shows how many volts you have going through the system, and it's a pig to read. Not only is it upside down, but it's back to front in a mirror. Duh.

Dave grinned again, opening his magic box of bits as Dad appeared to look at the bilge pump which had problems. Wiring problems. *Oops*.

After about twenty flushes of the water from the bilge, and a second pump installed, that one failed too, leaving Dave temporarily scratching his head and requesting that a goldfish be put in it so we could see the flow of the water out through the opaque pipe.

I went off in search of one, but only found a giant muddy carp, which didn't look amused at the thought. Instead, I just kept filling up the bucket for Dave so he could flush again.

I though putting goldfish down a toilet was cruel. It's actually a breeze compared with this.

All the while Dave worked he chatted about his boat that he lives on, which he is doing up over time as it caught fire a few years ago. Long story. We explained to him how we removed the fridge and are looking for a new one.

'I don't worry about that in winter.' He said, crimping a fitting to a wire. 'I keep my food in the canal.'

Dad and I raised eyebrows.

'You know, hang it over the side in a container, keeps it cold. I keep the rest of my food in the gas hatch in the front. Lovely and cold in there.'

We now know Dave's secret – quick picnic, anyone?

'I don't bother with heating if it's eight degrees or above. You get used to it. I live on the boat with my dog, we have great conversations.' He changed the subject quickly. 'I once bought a mower off a 79-year-old, even though I had three already. You've gotta watch these old people. They're deceiving they are.'

Another crimp and Dave hummed along to himself and chatted away merrily. He says he talks to himself and the dog a lot and apologised.

I do it all the time. Perhaps it's the ones that don't are the ones you have to watch. Earwigging someone talking to their dog reveals a lot about a person. Most people would think I need a straight jacket if they heard me.

After lots of hand wetting and pulling at wires, Dave decided he will come back next weekend to wire her up properly and get in a few other odd jobs (plus a beer or two at the marina beer festival).

Dad agreed and we chatted to Dave outside some more, whilst he admired our girl (I'm sure she blushed when he said how nice the roof looked).

He waved as he left in his little white van, and Dad and I tucked our girl in bed, looking back at her fondly as we too, left and said goodnight.

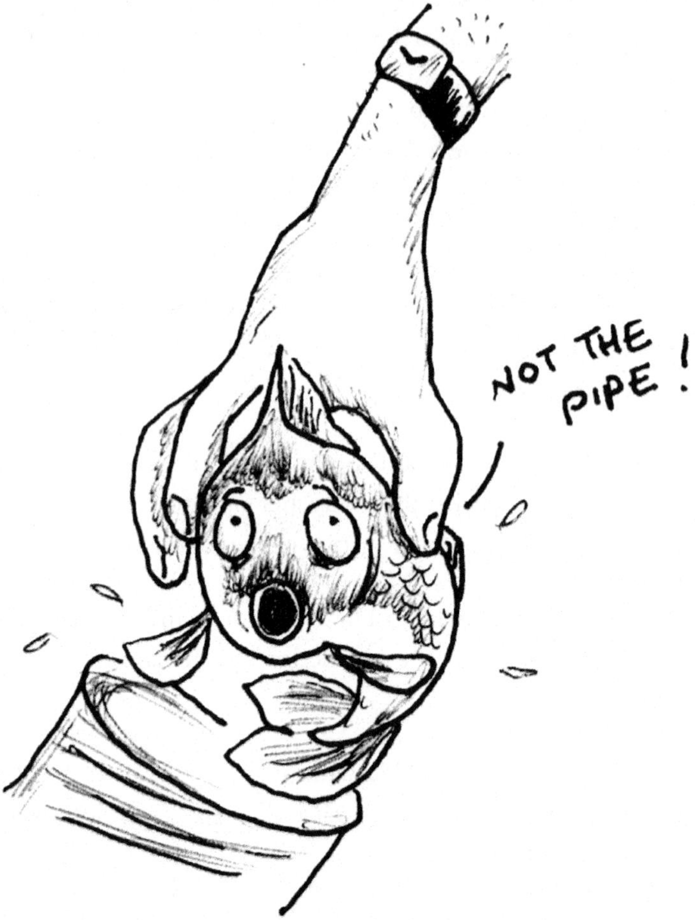
NOT THE PIPE!

30th August
Half Cut

Today started off bright and early. On the way to the boat to meet Dave our engineer friend, Dad and I conveniently arrived at the set of traffic lights at the same time as him.

Perfection (except the lights were red for him and he had to watch us wave merrily as we passed). And the cherry on the cake – sunshine, hoorah!

Whilst Dave tackled the bilge pump from last time, I fed the swans and ducks that clustered around the back of the boat.

All they had to hear was a rustle of a bread bag and that was it. It was like watching an aquatic scene from the film the birds in slow-mo, the swans rearing up out of the water to snatch slices and their broad bodies splashing back like monsters from the deep (pretty monsters).

They snorted indignantly as I threw the remaining crumbs over them, shaking my head. 'No more, sorry.' I have no idea why people call them mute swans, as they seem to have plenty to say if you refuse to feed them, even if it's on the grounds that you simply do not have a single scrap of food left on the boat (I'm a little over-generous when it comes to ducks, hence why the ones in the marina are like beer kegs).

Dave nattered away down in the engine pit and we listened to some of his hilarious stories, including how an old lady once touched his arse whilst he was fixing a light bulb for her in her house. Like Dave says, you've got to watch these older people.

At least on a boat your arse is nearly always up against a wall or an engine part, leaving little room for error or mistaken identity.

Dave grinned after fixing the bilge pump (it works a real treat now, and could probably empty the canal in an hour or so to give the Canal and a River Trust something to think about) and moved on to checking the antifreeze in the engine, which is at a level that could stand absolute zero (perfect for a relaxing winter trip across the North Passage).

The gas hatch came next – something I have never looked inside before, for good reason. Out came three gas bottles, a pond pump (the canal could do with the occasional water feature here and there – a fountain would be nice), several miles of hose, rust and, last, but not least, a fabulous pink foldable step stool that looks like a cross between Mr Blobby and a hobbit's high chair.

Incredibly proud of my finding, I stood on it immediately with a smug grin at Dad. These kinds of miracles are perfect for short people like us to aid in decorating ceilings.

After flapping the oven door open and shut for a few minutes, we discovered it had a mind of its own and the fan inside kept turning on and off. Dave looked at it suspiciously, threatening it with a screw driver. He found the plug underneath the oven attached to a socket on the floor (stupid place to put a socket on a boat where water sits), unwired it and ripped the oven out with glee.

Bits stuck together with grease like a complicated bowl of crunchy nut clung to the sides and ancient spillage stains plastered its back.

The oven attempted to have its own back and attack Dave with its door and hit him in the legs with a set of wire shelves. He laughed at it and threw it out on the bow where it stood looking miserable whilst we conquered the bathroom.

The new tap we chose in B&Q thankfully fitted first time (unlike the toilet seat) and Dave unscrewed the old waste with a cough and a grunt at the horrific smell that ensued. Black sludge went over the floor and I fled in horror as Dad took it outside with a pair of rubber gloves to dunk it in the canal and scrape it with a screwdriver.

Bravely, I poked my head back around the bathroom door to spy on Dave folded in half under the sink. I eyed up his huge tool bag on the floor, which he fondly described as a bag of 'useful shite'. At least it wasn't dirty shite.

Half an hour later, and we had the first new item on the boat fully installed, with a mass rush to use it to clean the grime from our skin.

With a scent of lavender soap, we were ready to take on the world and loaded up Dave's van with the oven and gas bottles.

His little dog grinned at us in an unfriendly manner over the front seats as Dave showed us a big red post knocker he had used to knock in over 70 fence posts during the week. I could barely lift it above my shoulders, so any fence I put in would just about hold back a couple of guinea pigs.

I leave those kinds of jobs to people with appropriate muscles and veins like rope wrapping their arms.

With a wave and a smile, Dave was off after a successful

morning's work and we rubbed our hands together in anticipation of lunch. Dad went off to pick up Mum and shortly after their return, we sat together munching through a cold picnic of scotch eggs and chicken slices, balancing plates on our knees and thinking longingly of the table yet to come.

The kitchen cupboards came off the wall shortly after lunch, with some levering and minding of the screws that had come through the bulkhead from the room next door.

After pulling down one kitchen cupboard, the central board of the ceiling fell down along with several unidentified items and a couple of dust bunnies, complete with their own grey lawn. Uh oh. Enough was enough.

At 2pm Dad and I wandered around to the marina office for the beer festival and to drown our (my) sorrows over the kitchen ceiling.

My keen nose quickly led me to the highest voltage cider which I clung to whilst chatting to some of our boating friends who also decided to join in the fun. We finally met some of our lovely neighbours who so far, we have only smiled and waved at, whilst they walk by with their little tiny dogs in jumpers. Yes, you heard right. Dogs in jumpers. Paste that image across your retinas.

Two of our friends we have known since the days we had a narrowboat chatted with us, merrily fuelled by cider and beer, their pink and argyle sweaters clashing together. The argyle was REAL argyle, worn by a real golfer who knows the name of every club and hole. That's some achievement. I used to think an albatross was a bird. Apparently it's a golfing term.

Half cut takes on a whole new meaning with a drunk boater, with one leg on land and one in the cut (cut means canal for non-boaters out there). I did wonder how our neighbours would manage to stumble back to their boats on the narrow jetty.

A live band turned up from Devizes, singing about how they bought a pint of 6X and carried on. Marvellous. If I bought a pint of that, I'd carry on somewhere else where there was more choice of drink, for a start. Bless them.

Some of the high voltage cider would give the band something to sing about, ooh-arr. Proper job, like.

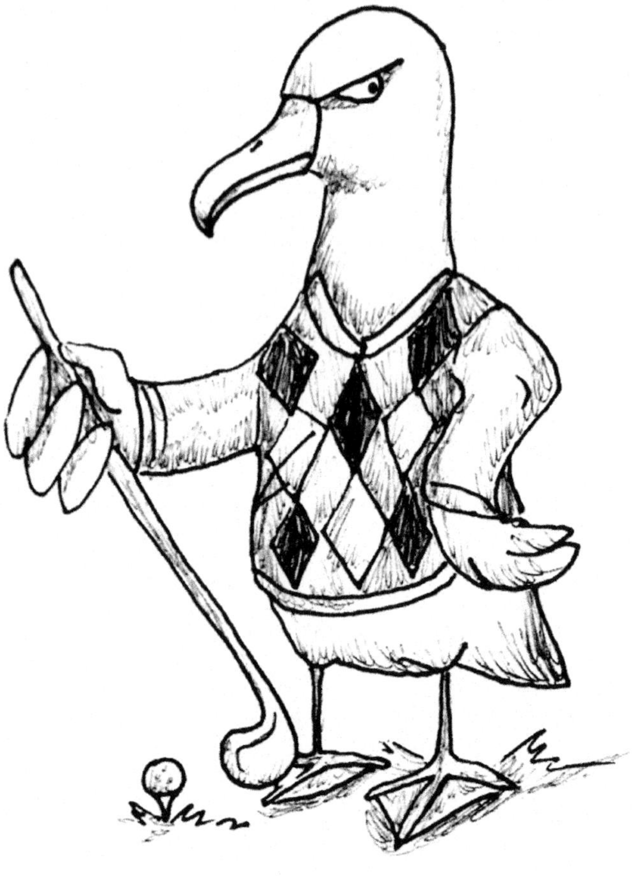

2nd September
A Simple Life

It feels like an eon since I last saw the boat, and yet, it was only a couple of days ago. Perhaps it seems that way because we all feel like we've been locked in the village stocks with bucket loads of tomatoes and other rotten veg thrown at us lately, what with work issues.

Life is so mixed-up, and tonight, Dad and I decided to take a trip up to the marina to see the boat. As we entered, we encountered people happily sat on benches together, or on the back of boats, smiling as we drove past to our allotted parking spot. It's a whole different world on the canal – much more peaceful, for a start.

Dad's first job of the evening was to check the radiators, as one of which had come loose from the wall whilst he pulled the carpet out from behind it earlier today – oops.

Hence the pile of paint tins, stools and a miniature step ladder propped against it to keep it upright and stop it from leaking.

Thankfully, Engineer Dave is due tomorrow to take a look with his trusty bag of useful shite.

Apparently, he is fuelled by a pint of milk and a Mars Bar each morning. If that can get you through hammering in 70 posts in a field with a tool that is half as heavy as a human, then I'm all for it – bring it on! It might help me become less sarcastic.

Dad stared wistfully at the roof, and within a few seconds, whipped out a roller and paint tin and slapped on another coat.

One whiff and I was high as a kite, wandering off with a big grin on my face to feed the swans at the back of the boat. They grunted and snorted in excitement of a treat, whilst every duck in the marina took to the air and landed in arrow formations behind them, carefully avoiding the long white necks with military precision.

There's something highly amusing about seeing a duck half-raising from the water, with its neck stretched and underside of its face and beak showing. I'm not quite sure what it is yet, but every time it makes me laugh. Either that or it's the smell of the epoxy-based paint, which is enough to make even the most sober turn hysterical.

The view tonight was excellent – long shadows, rolling hills, people arriving back to their boats fresh from work, the moon gently rising in the pale blue sky. Everything was calm and perfect.

Dad finished the back end of the boat whilst I watched the swans preening and flapping their wings.

Before long, Dad had finished and we went inside to clean up. I didn't need to wear a watch, as the neighbour's rear cratch has the most almighty clock inside that could rival Big Ben. From two moorings away I could easily see the second hand in its domed face.

They are rather kind to point it in our direction, a signal as if to say that time is ticking away permanently – oh yes, and Emmerdale is on at seven.

I watched a couple walk past to their boat with huge grins on their faces (it could only be the smell of the paint) carrying their shopping and clambering on board. Life is so simple here.

Before long, it was time to leave, and, after receiving several missed calls from a boating friend who constantly presses the letter 'A' in his pocket, we packed up and said goodnight to our girl, eagerly looking forward to next time.

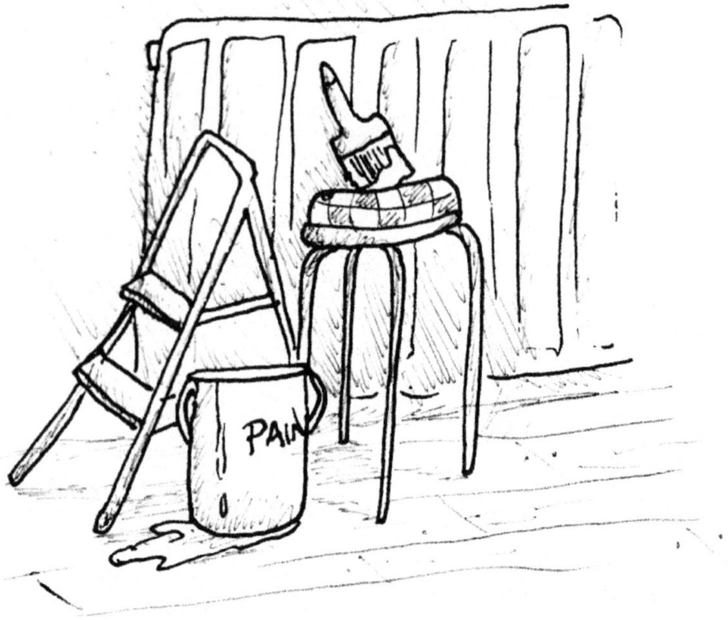
PAIN

4th September
Foul Play

There was me today, sat minding my own business at my desk at work, when an email popped up on the screen. From the marina. To dog owners. Perhaps there was a new fashion craze with dog jumpers I should know about. Click.

Apparently there's been a lot of dog owners not picking up their dogs mess (to put it politely), and the warning came. Click. 'If you are caught in the act, you will be removed from the marina with immediate effect'.

I'm not sure if that is meant to be aimed at the dog or the owner – either way, it should be picked up. It's not nice for us, or the marina managers, especially if your boat has cream carpets – and I did wonder about the funny stains on our mattress in the cabin.

If my dog crouched at the marina, there would be a disastrous effect, the equivalent of a Hiroshima bomb in dogs mess.

We need bin liners and shovels for our dog, being a Great Dane and all that. It's a good job we ask the dog to hold it in. Her arse muscles are like iron after seven years of training where best NOT to go. Hence the message has got nothing to do with us, but I stored the email anyway so I could remember to write this later.

Dad's been to the boat today and discovered that now, after the leaky radiator was kindly fixed by Engineer Dave yesterday, the other radiator is now leaking, so Dave will have to come back again on Saturday – he practically lives with us now. Soon he'll be keeping his milk in our gas hatch and mars bars in the bathroom.

The ceiling has also been fixed and now remains in place waiting for Mum to start painting – the green test swatches next to the window look like a modern piece of art. There may just end up a protest to protect them as a valuable piece of work by Banksy fans, so there could be some trouble before we get that far.

If a rich American wants to offer us a few million for it, then crikey, it's staying there. They can scrape it off and we'll keep the boat and the money – sounds like a bargain to me.

There's more plans to continue renovations at the weekend and the hint of a trip out – for now though, it's back to work. The weekend can't come soon enough.

6th September
Just in Case

We got to the marina extra early this morning in anticipation of Engineer Dave's arrival. As we drove around the corner to our parking space we noticed a van next door that looked suspiciously like Dave's, with a figure huddled in the back and a little brown and white grinning dog in the front.

How on earth he got in the marina without the gate code, we'll never know. Perhaps he was dropped off en route after the NATO summit by a chopper and airlifted in, like a scene from James Bond, Mr Obama giving him the thumbs up as Dave's dog's jaws were finally detached from his trouser leg.

The dog barked and I came back to reality. Perhaps he just parked up, waited and followed someone else in the gate, ramming them up the arse to get a move on.

He grinned and came inside our boat to fix the leaky radiator. Within minutes, all was sorted and the tea came to the boil – tea is a luxury when all you have is a toaster and a pair of rubber gloves that make up your kitchen utensils.

We all hovered in the living room, eyeing up the effects of the naked walls, now without carpet.

Ugly paper scrapings glared back at us, until Mum discovered we're missing some trims, which Dave will source for us. He said he'll bring his nail gun, and Dad nearly choked on his tea.

'What, so the nails go through the side of the boat?!'

Dave thought for a minute.

'I'll make sure to bring the short nails, just in case.'

That's some nail gun. I vote for standing on the other side of the marina when Dave does this, you know, just in case.

All done and dusted, Dave was off in a flash, and I grabbed a stool to watch Mum hoover the boat – our new hoover is a most complicated beast with a wheel in each corner and two holes. One to puff, one to blow. Instead of hoovering, Mum pressed the on switch and we were nearly blasted through the front doors.

After setting up a defensive barrage of a pile of books, I sat behind the doorframe on the bow, fingers in ears and counting down. Anyone who walked by on the jetty at that point walked even faster for fear of stopping to find out what was going on, or even worse, being signed up to a strange form of boat warfare.

Boringly, nothing actually happened and the hoover functioned normally, sucking the floor to death. No wonder there's a couple of planks missing here and there.

The boredom was soon replaced by horror, as Dad returned from the toilet looking flushed, I mean, FLUSTERED, slip of the tongue, wringing his hands.

The macerator had done to him what was (and still is) my worst nightmare. It refused to flush. And it wasn't meant as an ordinary or eco flush, either. You get the gist. We tried everything. Plugging in, then unplugging the shoreline, checking the inverter, turning it off then on again like a Windows PC (that logic doesn't work on boats I discovered) and pressing eco several times. Just in case. I couldn't find Ctrl + Alt + Delete either, so Dad wandered off in search of someone useful in the marina who told us to check the pop out trip switch.

YOU WHAT?

The pop out trip switch.

Oh. That.

The strange round thing that I always wondered about next to the switch board. As our switch board isn't labelled (except for a pencil mark on 90% of them saying 'loo' on the wood next to it), we've now discovered which switch is actually relevant. It's the 'turd one down.

I mean third, ahem.

Dad looked delighted that the toilet came back to life and disposed of any evidence.

We are quiet creatures that don't mind discussing other people's toilet humour, but prefer to keep our own, well – our own.

Unlike the people who walk by on the jetties with their cassette toilet in a wheelbarrow, which sets off Mum and I into fits of giggles every time. You just don't know where to put your face when someone walks by with their toilet. Should you say good morning? I know I have a damn job saying that with a straight face, that's for sure.

Mum gave me a huge family sized box of Shreddies this morning, and, hugging them with delight, I made my way to the back of the boat to feed the swans.

This giant, vitamin and fibre-rich pack didn't last long between

four swans and I managed to dispose of the entire box with them. They were, however, slightly despondent at the lack of milk, but enjoyed catching the hole-studded flakes that sank into the murky depths.

One day they'll dredge the marina and find that the entire basin is constructed from just Shreddies alone.

I'll have to ask Nestlé if they can hurry their Nanas up to knit more, especially at the rate these swans eat them. I know just how explosive fibre-wise one spoonful of these cereals can be, and I'd class them as dangerous to the people around you if eaten in vast quantities. Imagine what fun the swans will have tomorrow, propelling themselves around without the need for flight. Stuff Red Bull – with Shreddies you don't need wings.

I brushed off the remaining crumbs from the back of the boat and watched the swans chase each other around in a sugar-fuelled frenzy. At least they were happy.

A most entertaining thing is to throw a Shreddie at a swan and see if it lands on their back. If it doesn't, it bounces off with the most satisfying 'pop', which sounds like the swans are made from a crispy coated shell with a hollow inner. When it reached that point, you could tell I was hungry.

Super Dad came back from the marina shop with a packet of digestives and two bars of chocolate to keep us going whilst he watched F1 motor racing inside the boat. Mum and I sat outside,

feeling slightly buttered up. It was a tasty lunch, though.

After a pleasant morning of lounging and lunching, we got up to leave and prepare for our trip out on the canal tomorrow.

When I looked at the roof, I realised something. The colour is all well and good to dazzle narrow boaters coming the other way – but it also does the same thing to the skipper. It's such a glossy cream that the International Space Station could see us in the dark. And still get a good photo. Uh, oh. Sunglasses required.

7th September
Just for Fun

Hooray for no breeze and a marvellously still day for going out boat tripping. This morning we took off from our mooring to get to know the canal a little better aboard our girl, who today, behaved herself very well, with no naughty leaks or toilet problems.

Even the swans and ducks were still alive after consuming yesterday's Shreddies and delighted in eating half a box of Crunchy Nut as we left the marina today.

Ducks don't have teeth, so if you want a laugh, throw some Crunchy Nut at them, and watch their despair in trying to chew them. You can blame evolution for that one, not me.

The first part of the journey went well, and, pulling up at the swing bridge we decided to press pause and have a cuppa. One of our friends (another Dave) was moored behind us and came over for a chat.

We know so many Daves on the canal, including Glastonbury Dave, Solar Dave, Engineer Dave, Paint Dave and 'al' right Al' (he calls Dad Al') Dave, that I don't think my brain or Dad's phone book could store any more variations on that theme. My nickname at school was Dave. Lord only knows why.

This Dave (Paint Dave) came over to admire our girl's glossy roof and chat paint with Dad.

Paint Dave is very space-age modern with his own hydroponics bay at the front of his boat with green leaves poking out of the air vents on the side. We questioned the 'bushiness' and he grinned.

'I grow tomatoes and chillies – really hot chillies. Do you like them?'

I shook my head. Last time I had chillies I had at least ten pints of water next to me to wash it down with. And that was only the mild version.

Paint Dave patted the roof again. 'She's big, isn't she? She's like an aircraft carrier!'

Looks like next year we'll be painting a runway on top, in case the Navy need to practice inland waterway landings.

I'm sure our boat will be the butt (yes, big arse) of oversized jokes for months.

Kindly, Dave opened the swingbridge and we carried on, keen to get through the set of locks and down to the pub.

I sniggered at a narrowboat behind us that used a bow thruster to manoeuvre away from the drop off point. We've driven in 40mph winds and never felt the urge to use one. A bit of welly usually does the job. And a bump or two.

Before we reached the pub, Dad turned around above the final lock, whilst Mum clung to the TV aerial, desperately trying to stop the low-hanging willow from pinching her only link with Emmerdale. Never get between Mum and Emmerdale, it's dangerous, especially if the aerial is within reach.

Dad reversed into the lock, slightly disorientated at the peculiar sensation of using a lock back-to-front. Remarkably, he even reversed the boat into a mooring right outside the pub (you don't need to do it twice if there's a drink at the end of it).

He asked me to catch the rope on the bank and I did so with my teeth, the rope landing smack into my mouth. Dad asked me to catch it – he just neglected to say which body part I needed to use.

Shortly after mooring, Mum dished up a picnic lunch, and we sat out on the bow in front of the other punters who looked on as we ate in front of them, raising our drinks (from the pub, of course) into the air. Cheers!

There's nothing better than your own personal seat at the pub and your own decent dinner – no wonder the punters looked envious and disappointed when their dinner came out half an hour later. I'm not actually sure if we were allowed to do this in full view, but we did it anyway. Just for fun.

Our girl creaked on her mooring as if she had a bad case of wind, rushing backwards and forwards as boats flicked by in and out of the locks past her. The willow we were next to patted us on the head and got tangled in our rice puddings and jelly pots. We forgot to bring spoons with us (limited utensils, you see). Try eating jelly with a fork. It's not funny. Especially in front of others.

As I was about to tackle mine, the willow shuddered and a strange chap walked over to say he liked the name of our boat. He was dressed in bright colours and wore a leather pouch around his neck, which, Dad being naturally curious, asked what it was.

Apparently it was an amulet to keep nasty things like ghosts and ghouls away. We smiled sweetly at him and he disappeared, then rematerialised twenty minutes later and told us that the willow above us was rattling its leaves, so it was going to rain that afternoon.

Dad shook his head. 'Nah, dry all afternoon.'

The man said that trees don't lie. Fortunately this one did and it stayed dry.

We took charge back to the locks on our girl (after returning the pub glasses of course, don't accuse me of stealing them) and headed home.

I did consider perhaps borrowing some spoons long-term though.

A less-experienced set of narrowboaters asked if they could share the first lock with us. We raised our eyebrows and looked at them like one would eye up a strange beetle's behaviour under a magnifying glass, heads tilted to one side.

'You'll only have a few inches.'

They looked back, confused. 'That'll be okay, we don't mind.'

They didn't understand that we weren't on about the space in the center of the lock you would normally have between two skinny boats.

'No, we mean, literally, you'll only have a couple of inches, and you're just a bit wider than that.'

Their faces sank, then they realised their mistake and giggled.

It's impossible to be grumpy on the canal, even if you get it wrong.

Mum isn't fond of locks, so spent her time in each one as we went home sanding the railing in the kitchen to take her mind off of it, and ended up sanding off all the varnish in fear. I dread to think what might have happened if we had ascended Caen Hill Flight today. There wouldn't be a railing left.

Dad let me take control of the helm as we neared the marina, and two cyclists passed. One nearly fell off his bike doing a double take.

'Bloody hell, look, there's a girl driving that boat. That must take some steering!'

I just smiled back. Little did they know that actually, it doesn't take much steering and it's easier than driving a car. For me, anyway. You haven't seen my driving yet.

Spacial awareness can be a bit of an issue though. Apparently men don't think us women can park a car. Well guess what, I can park a fat boat – BEAT THAT.

At least on the canal everyone gets out of your way if you have a fat boat (don't worry, I always say thank you). Cue sarcastic wicked laugh.

Even fat boats get stuck in the mud, however, and under a bridge our girl's sixth sense alarmed her temporarily and she refused to budge, her propeller stirring up blankets of brown from the deep as if she had crapped herself in fear. I nearly did as well, forgetting that the gear shaft has more than one forward point and it could go faster. With a sigh of relief, our girl squeezed through the bridge and we made our way back to her mooring in the marina.

We stopped, exhausted and tied her up, patting her and emptying the other half of the crunchy nut box into an excited fray of swans who now turn their noses up at bread offerings. Sugar rocks. Bread's boring.

We patted our girl once more and left her cuddled up to the other fat boats, once again amongst her own kind and without discrimination amongst those other skinny boats. Bless her.

14th September
The Wild West

Going out on our girl is always great fun, but today it was made even more so by the presence of my brother and his lovely lady friend.

Before they got on the boat I handed them a paintbrush in a traditional ceremony. New guests have to wield the paintbrush with honour, that any scratches they make whilst driving the boat, must be painted over before leaving. If it's minus ten degrees, then as our guest, you'll have a long wait before going home.

They were both overawed by the size of the interior, squealing in excitement over how the bathroom was bigger than the one in they had in their flat. We apologised for the state of the unpapered walls and torn-out kitchen (the 'w' word has been keeping us all increasingly busy lately). My brother's eyes fixed on the sofa and his face turned from thought into bemusement.

'How did you get THAT sofa through THAT door?' He pointed at the small front doorway and we turned to look. It's a jolly good question. As the sofa was there when we bought the boat, how the previous owners got it on, I'll never know.

Perhaps DFS know the answer. I'll ring their customer service line in the morning and give them something to scratch their heads about.

I dread to think if we have to take it out one day. Either the sofa or the boat will have to be cut in half, whichever is easiest.

I know a few dogs that love a good chew on some leather – that'll sort it.

As we left the marina, we waved to one of our boaty friends who was frantically cleaning his golf buggy, a big grin on his face. I looked around, but couldn't see a golf course. Crazy golf, perhaps, with an extra large pond, a bridge and a few open windows as targets (the washing lines are great, especially when lined with nick nacks. If you hit a sock you score 100. A bikini 200. And briefs, well, that's up to the player to decide the score).

Out on the canal, we were met by an armada of boats travelling the opposite direction, like some mass evacuation from a disaster scene. We smiled politely at each one, only to look up the canal and see another on approach. By the eleventh boat, our smile was forced by sheer wind as our buttocks clenched on approach to the narrow section.

For the first time, we passed another fat boat, and our girl leaned towards her, eager to exchange a greeting. It was a little too eager for our liking, and we pulled her to the bank a little tighter to allow the other boat to pass without fear of harassment. We smiled, barely a hair's breadth away, and continued to the bridge ahead, where yet more boats passed.

As we neared the entrance of the curved brickwork, another appeared for a showdown.

Picture a wild west scene, fingers tapping on tillers, eyes squinting to see who was driving, the other hand revving the engine (with another eye squint, for effect of course).

The narrowboat ahead crumbled and pulled over out of the way, quivering as we passed with barely a fag paper between us to spare.

We said thank you and continued, leaving the poor thing refusing to continue for its skipper, trapped in the mud. We watched, sailing by as the people on board conjured poles out of thin air and started to push. Still their boat wouldn't budge. They were holiday makers after all. They needed the experience.

Just as we thought they might be stuck for the day and we would have to give them a hand, they were off again, their vessel shaken, but not stalled.

Finally, we reached our destination for lunch and we paused to moor behind a skinny boat which delighted in revealing all the places it had been with an array of brass badges attached to the back doors.

My brother saw things from our angle and laughed aloud at the size of their washing machine.

'Just look how teeny weeny that is!'

I looked at it and couldn't help but laugh myself.

It would just about do one pair of smalls at a time. If there were two of you on board with dirty underwear, it would be a disaster leading to an outbreak of civil war (big things start with something small, you know).

We ate lunch and pudding at the pub and strolled back to our girl, patting her and reminding ourselves how lovely she is size-wise.

People say boys like a bit of booty. I'm not a boy, but when it comes to fat boats, a little more booty is certainly better than them skinny things. (Don't call me politically incorrect, remember, I did used to own one of those, and I did love her). *Sniff.*

We travelled downstream towards the swing bridge and passed Paint Dave and Glastonbury Dave's boats. If all the Daves we know all moored up together, there would be no issue in remembering anyone's name. Just shout 'morning Dave!' and you'll never get it wrong. It seems 99% of the Daves I know live on the canal. Perhaps it's something to do with the name, who knows.

Dad turned our girl round in a flash, and got blown across the canal whilst I shut the bridge. Our girl wedged herself across the cut, so that our bow ended up right at a table on the towpath where two boaters were eating lunch. We grinned at them hopefully like strange ducks eyeing up what might be coming, but they simply raised their eyebrows and thought we were lunatics (it was stamped on their foreheads).

The journey back to the marina was wrought with even more skinny boats in the way (bless them), and even our marina managers who had sneaked out for a week on their own boat (I don't blame them) but we made it back in time to the marina entrance to avoid the lift bridge coming down as a car pulled up. We practically screamed 'whatever you do, don't put it down now!' in our heads to the people in the car. Either they saw us or read our minds, but thankfully, they decided not to drop it as we went underneath.

Safely back in her mooring, we tucked our girl in bed and my brother drove us home, smiling as he passed the other moored boats.

After an exciting day, it was only right to sit in front of the television at home to wind down before the onset of work in the coming week.

The trouble is, when you have a boat obsession, everything is seen from a canal perspective. At the London Palladium, two men danced on stage behind bath towels hiding their wares, and I had a vision of this happening on a roof of a boat. The audience on the opposite bank would have an interesting view, for sure. Especially as boats don't normally have baths, hence the lack of bath towels.

A flannel dance would be fun, I say, tut, tut.

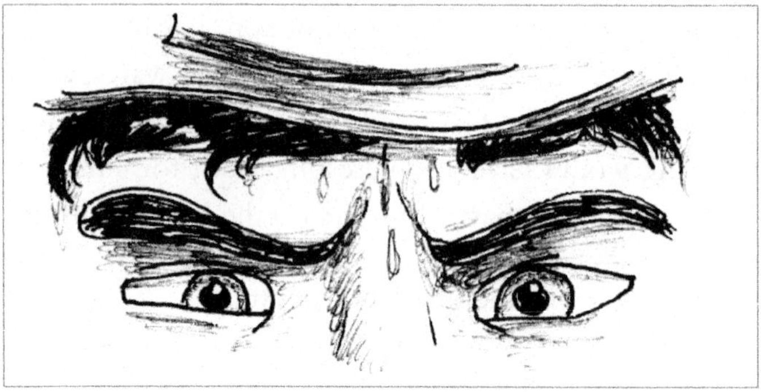

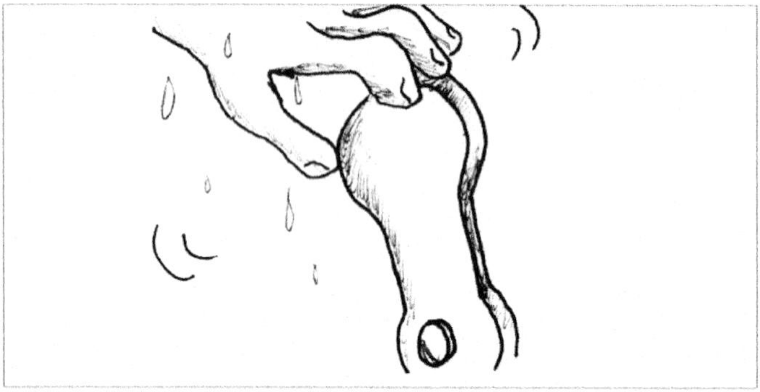

20th September
All in the same boat

The last few days have been exceptionally humid and warm for Autumn, bringing with them an invasion of daddy long legs which stick themselves everywhere from the ceiling to the shower and rudely stare at you through windows. Goodness knows how they don't slide off.

Sign Writer Rob (one of our boaty neighbours) apparently stuck himself in a similar fashion upside down on a marina jetty the previous night during a horrific electrical storm, hoping to catch a photograph of it overhead. I did some Google research regarding lightning protection on vessels recently, about how having a wired mast can create a 'cone of protection'. It didn't include a chapter about lying spread-eagled next to your boat with your arms in the air.

Today, the air was still and muggy with no hint of sun, (or lightning, thankfully) and we left the marina for a day trip with my Uncle and Auntie plus their two friends. We apologised for the state of the kitchen which currently houses half a tonne of cleaning materials, paintbrushes, sugar soap, kitchen paper and goodness knows what else on the work tops. How the kitchen units are still standing, I'm unsure.

Our family waved their hands and dismissed it, more interested in how the sofa got through the front doors. Everyone asks that. Even DFS doesn't know.

The minute we were out on the cut we met Paint Dave who had

wandered all over the place and was in a pickle with his boat.

We tried to negotiate to go around him the normal way (on the right-hand side), but after several hand signals and some confusion we had to go around him the opposite way.

Once we got closer we realised he was being towed along by a rope, whilst he punted merrily along almost on the verge of singing about cornettos. For a moment I thought we'd accidentally come out of the wrong marina entrance and ended up in Venice.

Paint Dave grinned at us.

'Engine blew up.'

We sailed by, pulling air rapidly through our teeth with a wince. Engines are costly problems.

'At least I'm going slow enough so you can admire my paintwork!' He smiled again and carried on punting.

It must be something to do with all the power required to keep his chillies and tomatoes warm in his hydroponics bay at the front of the boat. Either that or he decided to go one step further into space age technology and attempt a moon landing. Horsepower isn't designed for getting into orbit.

A fat boat behind him became terrified at finding themselves on the wrong side of the canal, confronted with another fat boat coming at them. We raised an eyebrow and looked closer. It was a Holiday Fat Boat, or 'HFB' as we like to call them.

These sorts are so buttered up by the free chocolates, champagne and the on-board jacuzzi (yes, you heard, JACUZZI) bubbles that they fear everything that comes in the opposite direction, including their own farts.

We smiled at them as we passed, raising our free builders tea and rusty windlass, feeling really hard. Bubbles? Pah!

The journey onwards to the locks was relatively calm, and we arrived at the first in the flight with a hoard of gongoozlers staring as if they had never seen anything wider than 6ft before.

'Will you fit in there?' asked an Australian.

I looked back at our girl, realising at the same time that everyone on board was wearing blue to match. We looked like a serious team effort.

'Only just', I replied.

The Australian looked concerned. They don't have canals down under because all the water would slide off, so they have good reason to worry.

One gongoozler was elated to see how a lock worked, as they'd never seen one in action before. Another looked horrified at my Uncle's bum cleavage, which naughtily revealed itself after strenuous effort to shut a stiff gate. That'll teach them to stare.

Someone else commented how clever locks are and that they could only be designed by a woman.

Last time I looked I'm sure John Rennie was a man. Either that or Wikipedia has got serious problems with its image database.

My Uncle and Auntie's friends asked how you tell when a lock gate is ready.

'Sit on it and you'll feel it lift under you. That sounds a bit rude, doesn't it?'

You can take that phrase however you want to, I'm saying nothing.

Once we got to the final lock to turn around, we got hijacked on the way out, and a little steamer boat overtook Dad and shot into the lock.

Within seconds, another boat wanted to come down. It looked as though we would be there for the day.

Having a fat boat means you cannot share with anyone (I don't like sharing, anyway), and hence you end up standing there doing the lock three times over before you can enter it yourself. And being late for lunch. And desperate for a pint and a pee (not at the same time, of course).

We even caught up the steamer boat in our earnest. The gentleman on it kindly held the gate open for us, and I congratulated him for not being racist against fat boats like everyone else seems to be. I didn't say it to his face of course – I just smiled and waved at him whilst he replaced his chimney after losing it in a bush.

Onwards we sailed before mooring up, and met our friend Terry the Paint – you guessed it, he paints. Boats, that is, not canvases.

My Uncle thought it would be amusing to give him a nudge with our girl as we passed and see if he could get Terry covered in paint.

Amazingly, every time we see Terry, he never has a spot of paint on him. If I paint, I have more on me than I do anywhere else.

Either he uses a magical brush, or I have an excitable twitch, one or the other.

A few gongoozlers strung around our girl, again bemused by her enormity.

It triggered off a row between Mum and a strange fellow who was absolutely certain our girl was bigger than 12ft and INSISTED it was so. Mum was almost tempted to get the tape measure out to prove it. The chap must have the same problem with eating – his eyes being bigger than his belly.

Being late for lunch and all that, we dashed off to the pub, arriving panting at the bar.

When lunch came to our table, I was intrigued that my Auntie's naan bread looked uncannily like a bicycle seat. Apparently it tasted like one too, but thankfully everything else was fine apart from the sausages. They were so overdone that throwing them at a duck might kill it, so I left them on the side of the plate so that the chef could use them to catch some ducks for his specials board. I hope he's a better thrower than Mum, or he might kill himself instead.

After pudding, we whisked back up to the canal and began the journey back to the marina. A skinny boat was having trouble staying moored, so we passed her gingerly whilst a kind gongoozler tied her back up again.

Unfortunately, even on tick over, our passing was enough to suck it back out into the canal again where it drifted across like a closing gate. The poor thing looked terrified.

We left the skinny boat sobbing whilst someone else on the towpath came to her aid, and continued onwards, my Uncle steering our girl with a big grin past some fishermen. I've heard that coarse fishing isn't to do with the type of fish. It's actually the type of language a fisherman uses.

A friend of mine taught me how to deal with this (not that I EVER will use this technique). He revved up his engine so much that a tidal wave from the rear of the boat washed the fishermen and their gear across the towpath.

Don't try this at home, and do not blame this book for any silly ideas you might have regarding fishermen. In general, they're very nice. Even if their smile looks as though they might be constipated – they probably are, after holding in their arse muscles, just in case they miss something when they go.

Back in the marina, our boaty friends waved us in and we were home, amongst the protection of fat boat corner.

Being in the marina is great and everyone is on the same level, or, excuse the pun, 'in the same boat.'

Our girl rested in her mooring whilst we chatted away the hours with a cup of tea, reminiscing of our day, and the light faded. Oh such a pleasure to go out on a fat boat.

Towpath Talk
October Special
How the Other Half Live

||||||||||||||||||||||||||||||||||||||||||||||||

Autumn brings with it the promise of beautiful hues of red and orange trees, the first whiff of wood smoke from a squirrel (the stove, not the furry creature clutching a cigar), and the smell of peaches.

Smugly waving his arms like a windmill, Dad recently set to work polishing one side of our new fat boat, covering it in thick, peach-smelling polish (yum) and taking half an inch of paint off at the same time. Apparently polishing is supposed to protect the outside of the boat for winter, yet somehow, it seems to have defeated the object. By 2016 we'll have a fashionable red oxide colour rather than blue. Still, anything's better than pink.

Inside, I've discovered just how dangerous Mum is with a bucket of water and diluted soap. I double-checked with the manufacturer and told them that they've neglected to write this under 'health and safety' on the sugar soap technical data sheet. I'd recommend steering well clear when the rubber gloves come out – even the ducks in the marina swim away at this point.

Thankfully, all this furious scrubbing hasn't bought the ceiling down again (don't decide to remove your kitchen wall cupboards single-handed without making sure how the ceiling is actually held up).

Our friend Engineer Dave kindly stuck it back up for us with a strategically-placed lump of wood. Next time he'll be coming with his nail gun to add the gunnel trims. Dad's still concerned that the nails will be too long and we'll be able to see daylight through the sides like some archaic punch hole knitting pattern. Fisherman's rib would look interesting.

Soon, we'll be waving goodbye to the cracked granite worktops in the kitchen, as Engineer Dave has his beady eyes firmly fixed on them. He's coming back shortly, hopefully armed with several buddies with muscles like tree trunks and exemplary ballet skills to remove them with care from our girl. What he's going to use the tops for, I daren't ask. Granite can be deadly in the wrong hands, especially his.

Weighing down a boat is a dark art, and any removal of heavy objects (particularly in the kitchen) requires precision, thought and forward thinking, hence we have been inviting everyone within earshot to use the bathroom as soon as they feel an urge coming on. Filling up the toilet tank is one way to achieve the perfect balance. Until you empty it and everyone falls out of bed at night and the kitchen drawers refuse to shut, of course.

As part research, part break from work, Dad and I recently stopped off for a visit to a fat boat café at Bathampton. I daren't tell our girl that this one had a bigger bow – she might get upset, especially with all the oversized jokes owners of skinny boats throw in her direction lately. She's a bit sensitive in that department.

The cakes in this floating café were enormous, coming in at a close second to the height of Caen Hill Flight. Whilst I tackled a chocolate one with glee, I listened in on a marvellous conversation about how the torso and legs of Lycra-clad muscled men look yummy framed in the boat's doorway (you can't see their heads as they have to duck down first). Someone behind me piped up: 'You can't really describe these men as mammals* really, can you?'

Someone else cried: 'Wouldn't you class them as gods?'

I snorted into my ginger beer, blowing bubbles and feeling rather like a common mammal. The ducks in the canal behind me thought it was hilarious.

Apparently the café was once subject to a hen party drifting by on a hire boat with 'butlers in the buff' on board, and there was a mass rush as the customers raced to look out of the port side, treading in ham paninis and almost tipping the boat over in the process.

In the marina where our girl is moored, the nearest we get to nudity is our neighbours taking their shoes off to go inside their boat. I don't think I could handle anything more exciting than this. Perhaps the closest we'll ever get is the marina manager not wearing his luminous blue braces, as he never goes anywhere without them.

I sighed into my glass of ginger beer, thinking longingly of our boat at home and looking down into the café interior at the Dutch barge-sized baguettes. My, how the other half live.

---

*I've since learned that the word 'mammal' that I overheard was one of a different type. According to the Oxford Dictionary, 'MAMIL' stands for 'Middle Aged Man In Lycra'. I withdraw the statement about feeling like a common mammal. I'm neither middle-aged, nor a man. This is getting complicated. Turn the page.

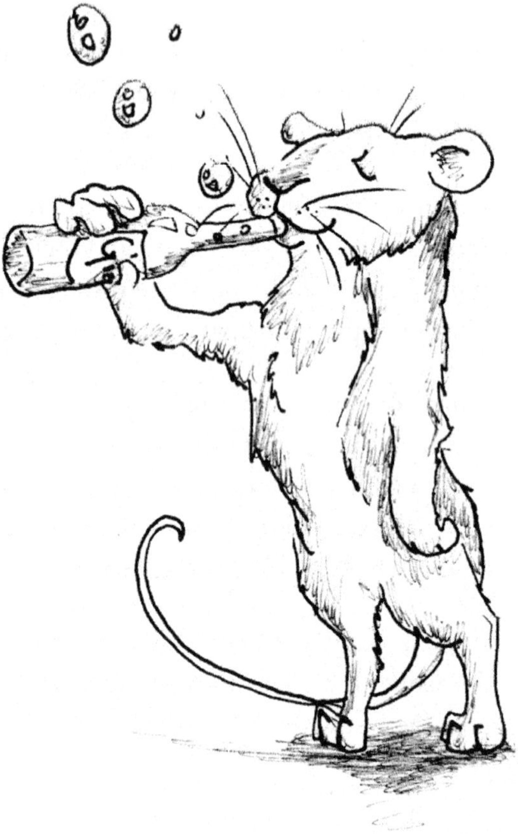

26th September
Messing about in boats

This week has been so busy work-wise, that it passed in a flurry and left me with withdrawal symptoms for our girl once more. I pined her chunky shape that skinny boat owners are so prejudiced against, and longed for her equally wide and comforting sofa.

I sighed with satisfaction yesterday when I was relieved of such longing by watching half-a-million pounds worth of boats whizzing up the Thames at Pangbourne.

After working in Reading in the morning, it was only right to grab some snacks from the local Co-Op and sit beside the river. For us, there's no getting away from the canal, or an adjoining river. We just love it too much. Our internal sat-navs are set as 'canal' by default destination. You have reached your destination – moor up.

No matter where you are, whether by a river or a medium-sized puddle, even the hint of a rustle of a carrier bag can summon ducks from half a mile away, and we were surrounded by more than a dozen of them within seconds as we sat down on a bench to eat.

We quickly scoffed down several muffins before waving the paper cases at them in surrender. They frowned in utter disgust – if you've never seen a disgusted duck, picture it as Mr Bean eyeing up something he'd never eaten before. You'll quickly discover ducks do in fact have eyebrows.

Thankfully, at that moment a lady with a child and a baby in a pram saved us from possible disaster by throwing a loaf of bread at them. A marvellous shot indeed, especially when you have a pram in one hand and a child in the other.

A crane chugged along nearby, coughing out exhaust fumes over the river as it turned to work on the newly-refurbished bridge which stood out, lily-white like a pair of lacy underpants across the water. Boats roared by underneath, diving in and out of the lock, creating bow waves that could rival the Severn Bore.

Fortunately, the ducks had remembered to take their seasick tablets the morning prior and rocked about on the waves with only a hint of green around their beaks. Or maybe that was the male ones. Either way, they still looked green.

The entertainment of the afternoon got even more interesting as a group of children came out of the activity centre nearby to dabble about in the colourful kayaks nestled on the river bank. We watched, a chocolate bar in hand and intrigued, as the teacher in charge told them to throw their paddles in the water, then 'go fetch' in the kayaks. My face was just as confused as theirs. Perhaps the teacher was an ex dog trainer. That would explain a lot.

After a few minutes, the children seemed to get a better grasp of what was needed to be done, and were happily scrabbling around in the water using their hands as propulsion. I only hope they remembered to take their seasick tablets before the next boat came along.

Mum has been busy this week painting the inside of our girl (I've yet to see it), and packing mugs for the weekend's 'tea on the boat' session. She always packs a spare in case someone happens to drop by. I dread to think if two people dying of 'tea thirst' dropped in.

One of us would have to share, and it would NOT be me. No-one else likes chamomile tea, anyway, so I have the upper-hand in these matters.

Not being the sharing type, I make it an absolute essential to deliberately forget to take the biscuit jar to the boat each week, instead, eating them all at home when no-one's looking. It wasn't me.

If you read that bit, don't tell Mum, she doesn't know who it is yet.

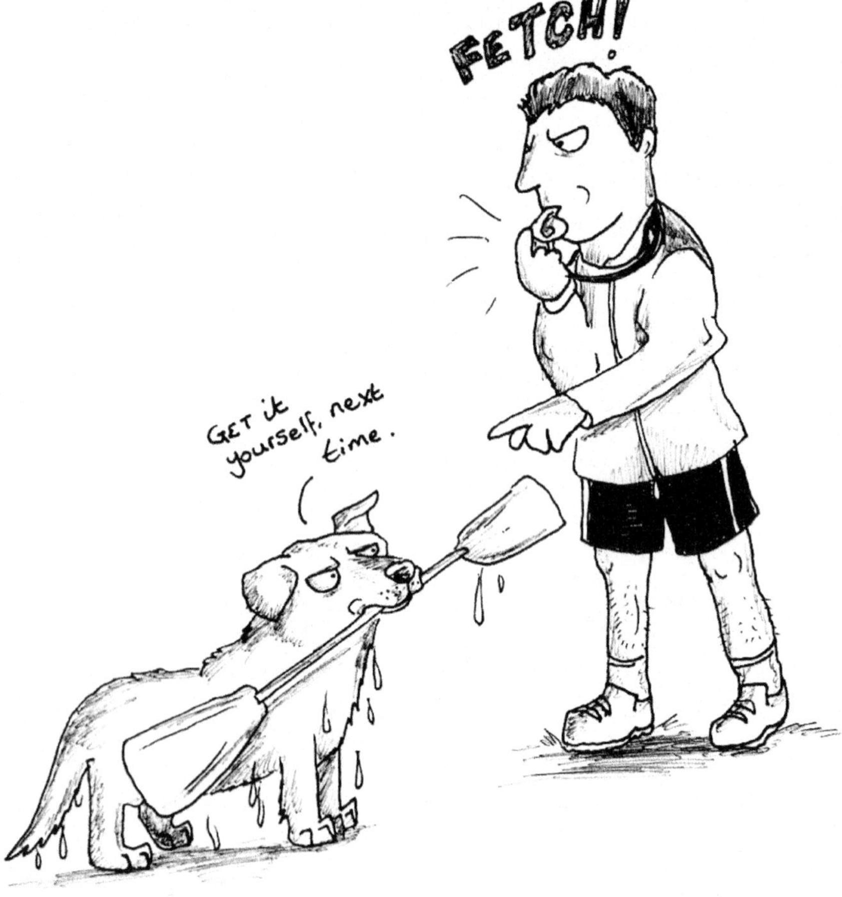
FETCH!
GET it yourself, next time.

5th October
Battle of the Bilge

This weekend started off wet and miserable, with heavy showers dampening our spirits on Saturday morning.

However, even a spot of rain couldn't stop Mum's tenacity with a paintbrush and the inside gunnels received a lick of green paint (the occasional splash of paint too, as Dad's and my impatience proved too much and our pacing caused momentary wobbles and a spattered finish on the floor).

After being threatened by a paintbrush, I was promptly sat on a stool and given two brass air vent grills to polish. Judging by their colouring, they had never seen Brasso in their lives, let alone BB cream (Big Boat cream, that's what it means, ladies).

This fancy new cream we have comes in a big white pot, and boy, it's better than any of that anti-ageing rubbish.

Stuff laser renewal, this cream can wipe prehistoric crud off of anything brass in under a minute (with a bit of elbow grease, of course).

With about twenty grill sections on each, it took over three hours, during which time my white apron had turned charcoal and I had to be fed biscuits like a duck – basically, open my mouth and hope who ever passes plonks one in. Squeaky 'feed me!' impressions work great and imply that you are suffering for a great cause – in this case turning dirty brass into gold. You could see me plus the biscuits in them when I had finished.

As the rain started to cease, Sign Writer Rob loomed up in front of our girl's doors and waved, a grin on his face. The water-stained windows amplified it. 'I've come to do your bilge!'

Dad showed him in the back of our girl, and there was a great deal of banging and scraping, after which I came to look out of curiosity.

When I peered over Dad's shoulder into the man shed, Rob brandished a bucket and a scraper with glee, his body contorted into an isosceles triangle and back propped against the hot water tank. He patted our girl's bottom. 'Oooh, she's warm.' He passed up the bucket full of her rusty shavings. He frowned. 'She's got a dirty bottom mind, I'll say that.'

Dad looked up and spotted the sun breaking through the clouds.

Sign Writer Rob carried on scraping. 'Wonderful, I can't see nothing down here, only engine bits and greasy things.'

It looked like Rob needed greasing up too, so I dashed off to the marina office to buy a jar of coffee, his shouts echoing in my ears.

'See if they've got carrot juice as well, will you, it might help me see in the dark!'

When I came back later, the paint tin had come off and our girl's bottom was starting to look marvellous. Mind you, anything looked marvellous at that point with the waft of paint fumes erupting from the bilge.

By the end of the makeover, we were giggling like chihuahuas on helium and anyone who happened to walk by raised their eyebrows and ran, in case the fumes caught up with them, too.

Rob walked slowly out of the bilge like a Halloween monster dripping with grey primer, hair encrusted and stood on end. Several big creases ran across him where he had been wedged like a ham sandwich next to our girl's mighty engine. Even an ironing board would have a job straightening him.

He ambled off for a shower and we headed home to relax before coming back the next day.

Our bilge can now dazzle anyone who happens to opens the hatch, and Dad stood admiring it in the morning, sunglasses on, before we set off for a brief cruise to the pub and back for some lunch. As we set off, a little bi-plane roared overhead and I laughed, undoing the ropes at the front. 'Chocks away!' Why I found it funny, I don't know. It must have been the lingering fumes.

We dashed off onto the cut and paused to eat our Sunday roast at the pub before turning back to the marina and mooring up once more to prepare our minds for the coming working week.

There was Sign Writer Rob on the jetty boards, grinning, his creases gone, and every inch of grey scrubbed off. He stood, shivering in his shorts and t-shirt. The autumn weather was starting to crawl in from the North.

The morning had been cold, and Rob had bought some celotex board to stick in his hatch above his bed, after being tortured by condensation dripping onto his face in the early hours. Apparently, there's lots you can do with leftover foam board and a tin of beans. How someone didn't discover the power of flight sooner we'll never know.

Beans, as always, turned the conversation naturally towards poo, and Rob turned his nose up at the idea of having a pump out tank.

When he and his lovely lady took on their narrowboat, the poo tank split, leaving them with a rather fetching mess, and years of fossilised dumps left from the dark ages which took several days of chiselling to get off of the floor. The tank itself had become encrusted to the ground, stuck like the glass case that surrounds the Crown Jewels.

We looked at Rob, horrified, then gazed open-mouthed at each other.

'I think ours is under the bed, isn't it?' Dad said.

Rob smirked.

'Just think of it – you're laying on three tonnes of sh*t!'

Aren't we all.

19th October
Best Behaviour

Winter's on its way, and, unlike hurricane Gonzales, work on our girl is starting to slow. Now with the interior walls painted and the bilge looking stunning, we've paused for breath.

This week was kitchen week, and off we trotted to the West Country to hunt for a kitchen somewhere cheaper than the big name stores. We ended up at a showroom in Taunton, and stood marvelling at the enormous bathroom displays (yes, the company does bathrooms as well as kitchens, not a million miles away plumbing-wise and all that).

I stared at a bath resembling a catwalk shoe and had to walk around the other side, just to see if it was real. It certainly wouldn't have fitted in our boat (or anyone else's for that matter, unless its name is the 'Ark Royal'). The water tank wouldn't cope, for a start.

And as for the tiles, well – that's what I call BALLAST. I've never known all four bathroom walls to be covered in more granite than the Cornish coastline.

The sales assistant pounced out of the kitchen department to greet us, and lead us around to gaze lovingly at coloured under-lighting, hidden pelmets, drawers that shut smoothly with a nudge (great for when other boats pass at 6mph rather than 2mph) and doors with no handles (meaning you don't become momentarily attached to the furniture when a holiday boater smacks into you and, in fear, your sleeve decides to hang onto something with a mind of its own.

Clothing sometimes has its own rational thoughts, which is a dangerous thing to contemplate).

Mum stroked the glass splash back. 'I'd like one like this.'

A sucking noise ensued as the salesman squeezed air through his teeth.

'Ooh, no, you can't have glass on a boat. Boats have to flex.'

Last time I looked our boat didn't have the muscle capacity to flex, and I'm almost certain there's something called glass in the window frames. Either that, or it's my imagination.

'It'll crack you know. I have a motor home, and I know what that's like.'

Depends how you drive it I suppose. There's no humps in the canal. Unless you find a bike or shopping trolley under a bridge. That's always entertaining.

'Come, come.' The salesman whisked us off to a large dining table and chairs planted in the ugliest kitchen display on this planet, with dark blue doors and light grey and black mottled work tops. The salesman waved his arms in between setting up his laptop.

'£24,000, this kitchen, you know.'

Mum and I looked at each other, eyebrows raised. Obviously, the uglier the kitchen, the more expensive it is to make. Good job we're getting a lovely shiny white one for a modest sum.

Our girl would not appreciate being ugly on the inside, it would be an insult. Blue kitchen units? No thanks.

Once we had settled up and chosen the extra hidden cutlery drawer (extra safety so it doesn't decide to randomly fling open when the poo tank is full), we made our way home, breathing contented sighs as we imagined what our girl will eventually look like with her new makeover.

We were briefly distracted by a traffic census and pulled over by the police to ask where we were going, where we had come from etc, etc. It ended up a life story and the census-taker was crying by the end of it, especially when we mentioned about the granola behind the oven that we threw off of the boat. That brings tears to my eyes, too.

Unfortunately, the census-taker failed to see me in the back (the glory of tinted windows) and assumed there were only two in the car.

I looked down at myself, just to check I hadn't sprouted a tail and fur in unusual places.

I tried to growl menacingly, but it came out all wrong, so I settled for a royal wave and a laugh, leaving the census team crying by the roadside about the horror of Sign Writer Rob's pump out toilet tank story. That gets everyone, that one does.

Later that week, we met our new boaty neighbours who came to claim the empty space between us and our other neighbours. I'm disappointed as I can no longer see the Big Ben-sized clock in their rear cratch, so have to rely on a watch instead.

The new neighbours on the other hand (no pun intended) are interesting. They have a fat boat (obviously, it's in Fat Boat Corner with the rest of us) and have come armed with packets of briquettes for their stove. Perhaps there's a cold winter coming and they know more than we do.

The gentleman works for the Canal and River Trust – better be on our best behaviour (or else) and the lady appears very good at cooking. Mum spied a whole trussed chicken awaiting to go in their oven the other day. It was already dead, mind, which proves they aren't suspicious or strange.

New neighbours – how novel.

We also have a marina warden at the moment whilst the managers are on holiday.

Walking into the office is like stumbling upon Dad's Army. All it needs is the warden to wear a white helmet with a 'W' on.

Mum and Dad dropped off some fresh, home-grown grapes from our garden the other day and he took them with a smile and replied: 'that'll perk the troops up!'

He does, however, do a marvellous job for the managers and the marina is certainly staying perky.

It might also have something to do with the mammoth pile of chocolate bars and strawberry fizz laces on sale. There's nothing like a strawberry lace to get motivated. Or in my case, a whole packet works wonders for driving everyone else up the wall.

Towpath Talk
November Special
Fatal Attraction

The interior of our girl is finally starting to take shape, what with Mum's exceptional wallpapering skills and fastidious painting.

Never before have I witnessed such skill in cutting straight lines, especially when someone (meaning me) had the attack of the fidgets after eating an entire 150g bar of Turkish delight in one go. The effects of E numbers aren't just for children to enjoy, especially when you have a 12ft-wide boat to race backwards and forwards across.

Thankfully, Dad can't see any of the bits I missed the other week when I cleaned the brass mushrooms, as he lost his posh reading glasses (guess where, *splash*).

Shortly after, he cunningly devised a complex system of crocodile clips, wire and super-strong magnets to go fishing with in the hope of retrieving them. After a few fruitless dunks, an excited look crossed his face as weird, grungy treasure emerged. Out came a metal bucket and a huge hand saw a lumberjack would be proud of (caught by the tip, of course).

If you happen to find his glasses, they used to have white arms with 'Red or Dead' written on them. Judging by the time they have been submerged, the arms will be orange and the label will say 'Brown or Drowned'. Mum has a mental image of opening the blinds one day and seeing a duck or swan emerge from the water wearing them. Very fetching.

The magnets on Dad's fishing device are so strong, I'm starting to wonder if that's the reason that all the other boats around us don't move from their moorings. I dread to think what happens if they suddenly need a pump out – we'll have to hold their hands when they go. I think it's called fatal attraction.

Mystery Neighbours

We like our boaty neighbours, Sign Writer Rob and his lovely lady, for one very good reason. They described our girl as a *Ferrari*. Wow. Everyone else just tells us she's huge, a monster, a beast, the sort of thing that gets in the way. Apparently it's to do with her shape, which Rob fondly described as 'wide and low'. She's also wide and slow, thankfully, or she may well cause serious problems on the canal with washing fisherman off of banks and the like.

Rob's boat is one of the skinny fraternity, with a chug-along Lister engine – the sort that the person steering it has to don goggles, a flying helmet and a stiff-wired scarf (there's hardly any breeze when travelling at 4mph, hence the wire for dramatic impact). Rob's other name is Biggles.

The marina has a great community and social life – it's like being on holiday. I actually even saw someone wearing a Hawaiian shirt once.

Often, Dad and I go off on a mystery tour whilst Mum does the wallpapering. The jetty boards zigzag all over the marina, and you have absolutely no idea who (or what) you might encounter next.

On our last tour, we could smell gravy at the back of one of the boats. We only had to lick our lips and our friend Ian pounced off of his stern to proudly tell us he and some friends were having a huge roast pork that evening.

How on earth they got it in the oven, we'll never know – that's the reason we call our tours 'mystery'.

Waving goodbye, we decided to wander in the other direction towards the marina office to buy some supplies. We passed a boat called 'Guinness', whose owners were painting a frothy white stripe along the top of the black side panels. At that moment, every fly in existence got stuck to the fresh paintwork, and their boat ended up resembling a packet of garibaldi biscuits. Another mystery.

Eventually, we made it back to our girl and flopped out on the jetty boards to feed the swans with a family-sized box of Shreddies.

I buy the swans their own pack and I'm sure they are delighted. So is the supermarket, even though they look slightly suspicious as I pass the checkout with a bulk-load of boxes in the trolley. I've put in a request to the Shreddies Nanas to hurry up and knit more, as there will soon be a world shortage.

We'll have to get the kitchen sorted soon, or there may well be a shortage of cupboard space, too. Keeping mugs in the wardrobe is a bit awkward, especially when you have guests. They just don't understand.

9th November
A study in sparkles

The cold North winds have returned to remind us that it is actually the end of autumn, and the rain has followed suit to make everyone feel equally Novemberish. Yesterday's extremely brief trip to the marina to see our girl was no exception. It was the usual case of Sod's law, the sky opening with impeccable timing the minute we stepped out of the car. Marvellous.

Dad stood fumbling with his keys to find the right one for the lock, whilst I stood huddled against the wind watching the swans and ducks who looked overjoyed at the prospect of water beneath them and above them at the same time.

Miserable and shivering, we clambered aboard to gaze upon Mum's remarkable wallpaper feats from earlier in the week, in preparation for the new kitchen arriving very soon. Mum has the extraordinary power to wallpaper over anything and still retain a perfect straight line.

If the dog happened to be leant against the wall, it would be easily papered over with only the tiniest bubble visible (at the arse end, of course). I dread to think what would happen if Dad or I stood still too long, hence we steer well clear and leave her to it.

The weather has turned so chilly that the PVA glue Mum has used to seal the woodwork on one wall hasn't yet dried from several days ago, and, as a consequence, anyone who happens to wander past realises they no longer have a jacket on, the wall seizing it from their possession and automatically hanging it for them. Who needs a coat peg?

It's now become a fashion inspiration wall, featuring the very latest trends, as well as a few 'model's own'.

Dad whipped out a tape measure (before the wall grabbed it) and started to measure up for a set of window blinds, tripping over the tables, buckets of paste and hairy, mice-like rollers that have exploded all over the lounge area. It's like a supernova at a DIY store.

Well, since the granite has gone from the kitchen, we need something to weigh the boat down.

Mum is already planning the bathroom, changing it from white tongue-and-groove walls to black panels with twinkles in. Yes, you heard. Don't laugh.

Mum thinks the toilet seat should match, if we ever find one that actually fits, that is. Soon, there will be a graveyard of loo seats, and we'll have to glue them to the wall like taxidermy trophies.

If guests from Antiques Roadshow happen to drop by, 'ooh, yes darling, this was an original Victoria Plumb. Look at the finish – such – errm, oh, I didn't realise the underside came in that shade...'

We're going to go for a sparkly one. The current one is horrific (hence the hovering manoeuvre when it comes to ablutions), so what better way to treat your bum than with something that not only sparkles with cleanliness, but has twinkles in it to match the walls.

I wonder if they do twinkly toilet paper to match. It's bad enough for me to get two pairs of socks out of the drawer the same each morning. I don't think I could stand much more coordination without the risk of physical implosion.

Still, Dad is happy as Santa has come early with a little sign for the back of our girl with 'Man Cave" on it. It's the nearest we could get to 'man shed', which, incidentally, is soon to be painted gloss white to hide the dirty tide marks our girl has made up the wall from her greasy engine bits. My theory is that it will just show them up even more, but everyone else's is that it will get cleaned quicker. As long as it doesn't have twinkles in it, I don't care. Glue might be helpful, though, to stick random tools and bits of fluff to it, when not in use.

We clambered off the back of our girl and into the wetness once more, taking in the scent of woodsmoke from our neighbours who were huddled up inside their boats, not daring to look outside for fear of a soaking.

For a moment, I didn't blame them. They were all inside, snug and warm like hibernating bears.

The marina is incredibly quiet in winter. Everyone vanishes – until someone shouts: 'tea, anyone?!'

I do wonder sometimes what they're all up to in their little floating castles. I doubt they will be looking up twinkly toilet seats on their iPads, somehow. Maybe I'm wrong. They're probably reading this.

Today, however, the tables turned and the sun burst from wherever it was hiding yesterday. On a whim, Dad and I decided to hop on our bicycles and ride four miles to the marina.

After not riding one for several years, I became something of an embarrassing sensation on the towpath, struggling to keep up to speed and wincing at puddles (I don't have a mudguard, you see).

With a strained face, tight arse and a wide, somewhat wobbly berth, it was a job avoiding those loose hairy things called dogs.

Hills and bridges are also currently a no-no, inviting an incredulous dance at each one to jump off and on again. Super Dad had it covered and was off up the towpath in Wiggins gear (gear 26, if you have the good fortune to have that many).

When Dad cycles it looks like a walk in the park. When I cycle, I look like a first-timer at boot camp. Especially as my gears are seized up and stick in one position. Try climbing a hill in six, yeah.

Wobbling like a jelly, I collapsed onto the front of our girl and amused myself by watching our boaty friends who had broken their contract of hibernation and were out walking their dogs and catching fish (not at the same time of course – I don't think even a Newfoundland could manage that one).

We watched in awe as a neighbour caught a leviathan from the swirling deep. The shiny beast of a carp flopped about and bounced around his stern, only an inch or two away from smacking him in the face with its tail.

Our neighbour took it as a compliment and hugged the eighteen-pounder like a teddy bear whilst others around him snapped pictures. The fish smiled sweetly to the camera before flapping out of the cuddly grip and landing with a whale-like splash back into the canal. Stuff Loch Ness. Caen Hill has got bigger, huggable (if slightly slippery) beasties.

Sadly, as we do not currently have a kitchen, there was no such thing as a cup of tea on our girl, let alone a packet of biscuits, so we retired to our bikes and cycled past another neighbour, Colin, who eyed up my saddle with suspicion and fetched some tools to raise it.

Apparently, it seemed I was sat on my arse, no wonder going uphill was such an ordeal.

I love the suspension on my bike, and now Colin does too. I'd better not leave my bike lurking around, or there won't be any of it left. He's welcome to the front brake. It sticks and needs a flick to turn it off. Hah! Quick getaway? No chance. Not if I jump out in front of him.

On the way home, I was blessed by countless stops to catch my breath and chat to fellow boaters who eyed Dad and I up, slightly concerned for the lack of a boat. Apparently, we look totally different on land. At least a boat doesn't give you a sore arse.

Our boaty friend Terry the Paint surprised us with the news that he will be painting his boat black and orange. I thought orange was the new black – supposedly having both colours is a fashion essential. We'll be able to see Terry coming a mile off soon. Let's hope he doesn't go for tiger stripes, or we'll have to call him something catchier, like 'Tigger Terry'.

Still, at least he hasn't requested sparkles. There should be a law passed that the decor of your toilet must absolutely NOT, EVER match the outside of your boat. NO.

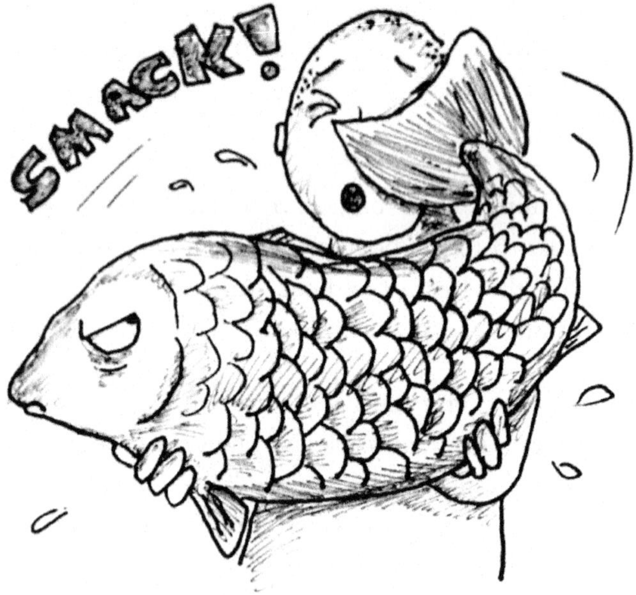
SMACK!

Towpath Talk
December Special
A Christmas Cringe

Extreme Measures

One word. You know exactly what I'm going to say. Christmas.

Being the first one with our new girl, we've decided that, as tradition suggests, to get a Christmas tree for her.

I'm usually the one who savours the task of buying the biggest tree possible and stands back to watch a lot of huffing and puffing as it is wedged every angle under the sun to get it through the house door. The usual result is the bottom being cut off so the tree doesn't form an arch under the ceiling. (My motto is if you bought it, flaunt it).

This year, Dad decided it was his turn to choose a tree for our girl. Mum and I left him to the responsibilities of shoving the monstrous fir through the tiny front doors, and came back from a brief walk to discover that his 'measure twice cut once' policy had blown away in the wind with the sawdust chippings.

Our mouths dropped open as Dad put his chainsaw down on the bow. There was no sign of the tree, all bar a one-foot green thing shoved into a pot that cringed at its own baldness.

The tree and I stared at each other for a moment. My eyes wandered over its bristly green branches.

Gingerly, I added a bauble or two and a bit of fluff, and, hey presto! It looked Christmassy enough. It's certainly better than nothing.

I whipped it from the gas hatch and smuggled it out of sight and inside before any of our neighbours could get any competitive ideas. So far, I believe we have the biggest tree in the marina, but don't tell anyone. We might have to take it home, being such an embarrassment.

I've heard rumours of mistletoe being strung across neighbouring boat doorways in a seasonal ploy. I'm not falling for that one. I choose friends wisely in December.

As for mistletoe at the marina entrance, I'm all for it. I'd like to see a narrowboat attempt a kiss with our brobdingnagian girl without being flattened like a piece of tin against the banks of the canal. I think she might pass on meeting a Dutch barge, though.

Tiny Turkey

As all the TV adverts say, getting a kitchen delivered for Christmas is fabulous (so you can wreck it cooking the turkey and throw wine over unwanted guests), so we've also opted for this policy, with our girl's new kitchen due very shortly. We might have to skip the cooking the turkey part though, as we no longer have an oven. If anyone has yet bred a turkey smaller than a Chihuahua, and it can fit in a microwave, you'll be instantly added to the Christmas card list. And maybe invited for a sandwich (saves on cooking all the trimmings and other things).

We're a little worried as we saw our neighbours with a whole trussed chicken on their worktop recently. That's some competition.

Mention the words 'new kitchen' out loud in the marina, and you find yourself with everyone who hears round like a shot asking if they can come on Christmas Day.

It's a good job Santa doesn't have to ask everyone. (We've put 'Santa stop here' signs on the roof of our girl, just in case. Being 55ft long, she's just a touch too short, so we've clearly marked the end of the runway with glow-in-the-dark mooring rope bands. I'd hate Rudolph to miss and end up in the drink).

How Santa will fit down the stove flu, I'll leave that to your children's imagination.

Our friend Engineer Dave relished the words 'new kitchen', and came to help rip out the old one.

Carrying off a slab of granite weighing more than the Tintagel coastline was a trial, and thanks to the aid of another new friend (Super Chris) and some ten points *Strictly* skills, it was carted off in a jiffy, our girl rising to the surface like a blue whale with a sigh.

Somehow, everything inside now seems decidedly wonky. I'm adding a spirit level to my Christmas list. And some crispy new oil filters for our girl's dirty bits. And a ten-foot barge pole (no, honest, it's not to keep our boaty neighbours away). And a new toilet seat that actually fits. We do this thing called hovering which is a bit uncomfortable, so it would be a wonderful gift for life. A toilet seat isn't just for Christmas, you know.

Joyeux Noel!

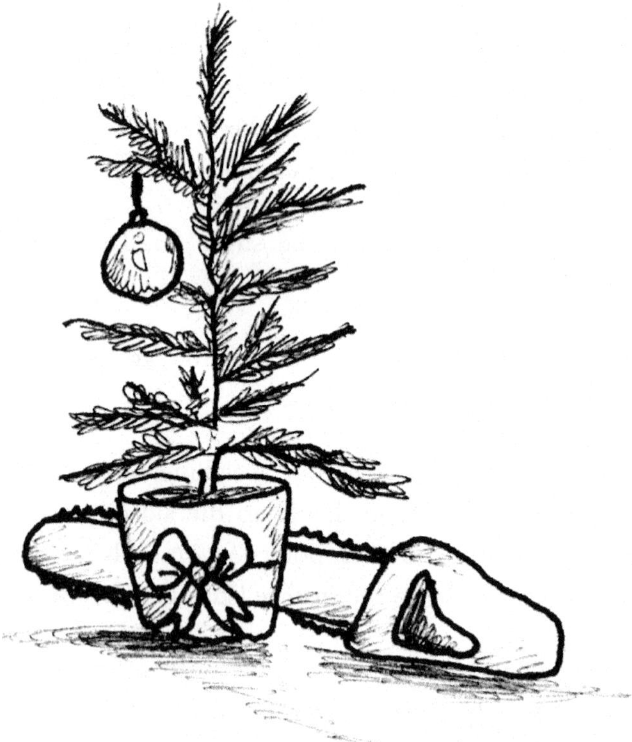

Towpath Talk
January Special
The Curious Case

We don't worry about the winter weather on our boat. Mum can tie a boat up with hurricane force knots that take half an hour to undo before casting ashore (there's no way we're letting go of our girl in high winds), so for the Canal and a River Trust to send a boaters guide in the post was an interesting gift, to say the least.

Just before Christmas we received this marvellous pamphlet which describes every applicable knot under the sun, plus an interesting story about a man, a curry, and a fire. No, it doesn't turn out the way you might think.

I'm too embarrassed to ask our boaty neighbours if they got one too, in case they roar with laughter at us and roll around on the floor. Perhaps CRT think our knots really are dangerous. Or that we might have an urge to block all of our air vents with biscuits. Or invite our guests to stand on one side of the boat doing the conga. Either way, it's a useful reminder to not go and have a curry whilst leaving the boat unattended.

Murder Mystery

Although our girl has been with us for four months, we're still discovering new things every time we open a cupboard door.

This time, Dad lifted up the double bed support to inspect the poo tank below and was confronted by a suitcase. Intrigued, he pulled it out and unzipped it slowly.

Did it contain money, perhaps? I watch too many episodes of NCIS and indulge in far too much Sherlock than is healthy, so my first thought was – 'what if there's a body?'

Dad continued to unzip, shaking slightly from the suspense.

To his horror, inside the suitcase was yet another suitcase. He unzipped the Russian doll-style secondary receptacle with caution, only to find a photo of a grinning man.

No money. No terrifying contents. No ransom note. Just a photo of a happy someone who obviously looked pleased at the thought of being such an anticlimax. Even Sherlock and Watson would have been stumped with this case (pun intended).

Disappointed, Dad wandered off in search of afternoon tea and Mum smiled at him from the bow.

'I know how much you don't like blueberry muffins, so I gave yours to the swan.'

The swan paddling by gulped, a cake-shaped lump in its throat, which slowly travelled towards its arse.

There was no chance of getting the muffin back after that.

Swearing blind

The disappointment didn't end there for Dad. The newly-fitted roller window blinds were having a little tension troubles with their springs and refused to automatically roll up after spending their first chilly night on our girl.

Amusingly, after a fiddle with a metal rod and a plastic pin, we got one of the blinds to work upside down.

Instead of automatically closing, it automatically opened. I didn't think this was even possible, and spent half the morning playing with the novelty, until I realised we had wound the spring up the wrong way.

There was nothing resembling instructions in the immediate locality, so it became a situation of the blind leading the blind and lots of swearing until, eventually, we twigged it.

Now the blinds zip up to the top of the window so fast, you have to be careful of wearing loose clothing next to them. Ties are enormous fun – I can't wait to invite an estate agent over for a cup of tea.

All of our blinds are custom-printed with photos on, and for the bathroom I've opted for something a little wilder and have designed my own fabric with Arctic Terns all over it facing in opposite directions to one another. Dad's eyes went in the middle when he saw them, and he clutched his head, claiming he had a funny 'tern'.

Tension trouble

Our bow fender has also been playing a somewhat confusing game as of late. Being too high up on the nose of our girl, it not only sees to make her look snobbish, it also misses every opportunity to protect her delicate undercarriage from bumps and scrapes (don't tell CRT if you see any missing sections of towpath).

Hence Dad and I trundled off to Victoria and Spencer's Boatyard to find some chain to lower it. Victoria has suggested tensioners, which, in theory, you're meant to have two of.

Dad scratched his head, confused. I can't wait to watch him fit them. It'll be like watching DIY SOS.

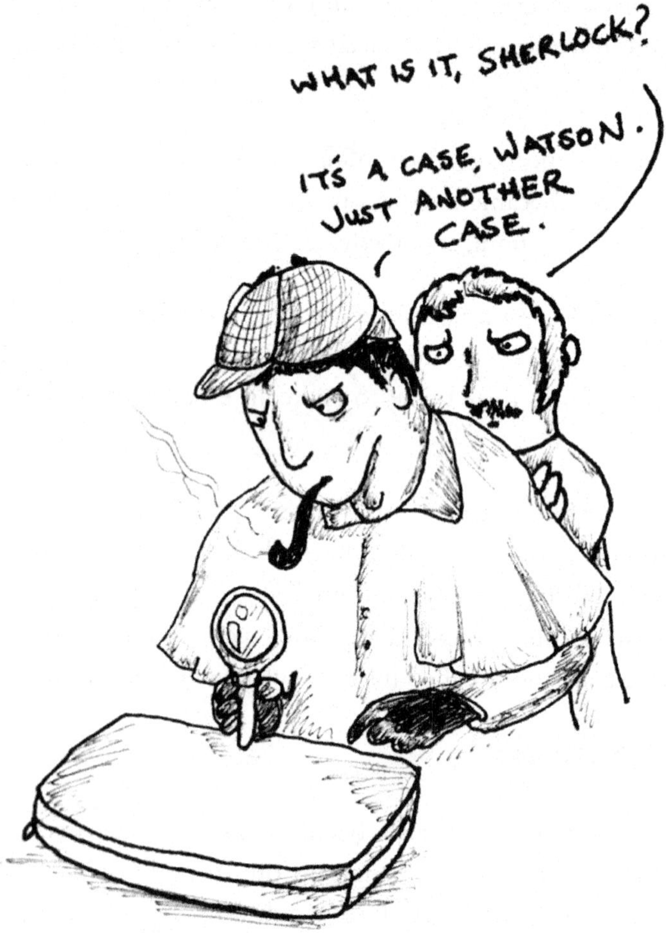
WHAT IS IT, SHERLOCK?
IT'S A CASE, WATSON. JUST ANOTHER CASE.

November 2014
The Fat Boat Handbook

|||||||||||||||||||||||||||||||||||||||||||||

In celebration of the release of the Canal and River Trust's new 'Boaters Handbook', I thought I would share with you the Fat Boat section which, unfortunately, didn't make the final cut.*

Useful knots

Hurricane force knot:

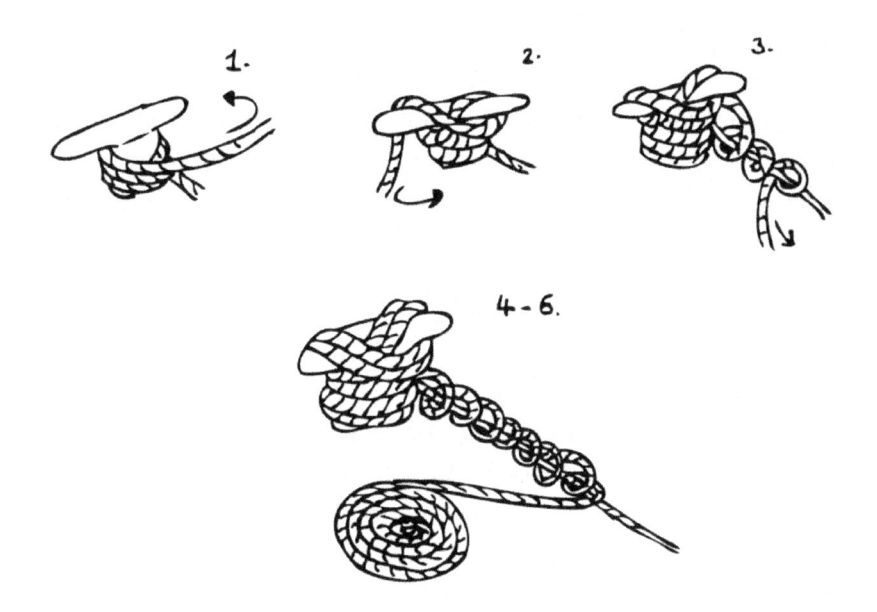

1. Wrap the rope twice around your hitch.

2. Complete a full figure of eight (over and under) your hitch, then wrap around twice more.

113

3. Tie three half-hitches.

4. Wrap a half figure-of-eight around the hitch.

5. Add another four half-hitches.

6. Trail the remaining rope and, holding the end of the rope in your left and rolling it gently, coil it into a decorative spiral to finish off.

Atomic knot:

Repeat the above steps 1-5 twice over, adding an extra two half-hitches before proceeding to step 6 if any rope remains.

Quick-release:

Loop the rope through the mooring ring or pin, and stand on the stern, holding tightly to ensure the boat does not drift outwards. To release, wait until your skipper asks you to cast ashore and simply let go of the rope.

Slip knot (quick-release variant):

Perform the actions as for the quick-release knot above, this time standing on the towpath. This knot is so called because of the dangerous aspect of the operator slipping on wet grass, dog turds etc. Be warned.

Mooring

If you plan to stop for lunch and anticipate you would like to continue afterwards to your evening destination, be sure to plan ahead. Remember that adequate overnight stay moorings are few and far between and require forward thinking to make sure your journey is stress-free.

Before mooring for lunch, consider the direction of the general flow of traffic on the canal. If the majority appears to be taking the course you will later follow, moor up in the bridge style as described below. Otherwise, moor up in the standard manner, using mooring pins if required.

Bridge mooring:

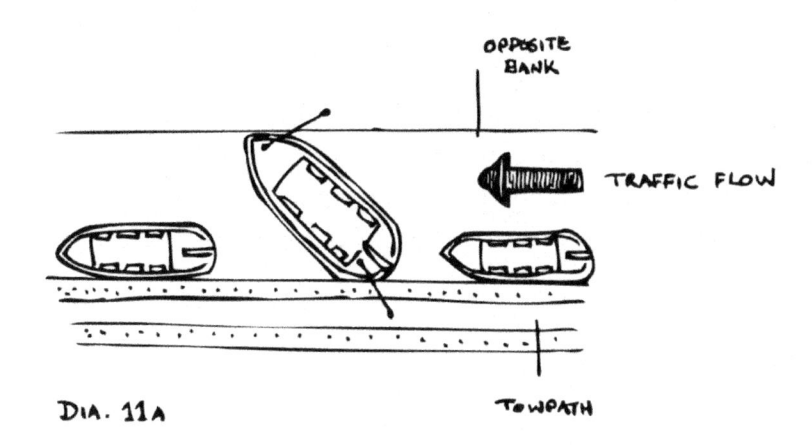

DIA. 11A — OPPOSITE BANK — TRAFFIC FLOW — TOWPATH

Gently pull up in the centre of the canal using a small amount of reverse to come to a full stop. Push your tiller hard over to steer towards the opposite bank and initiate full throttle forwards. Your bow should touch the bank, and your stern should be on the towpath side (see diagram 11a). Tie your stern rope to the nearest available mooring ring, and the bow to a mooring pin (or two in the double-cross position for added strength).

You should be able to step off of your stern and onto the towpath and rest assured traffic will be unable to pass whilst you have your lunch, thus potentially securing a mooring for the evening with little fuss.

Passing other craft

At max twelve foot wide, fat boats can choose either side of the canal to travel. If a craft approaches you, it will nearly always stop to allow you to pass. Always say thank you to the crew and, if possible, reassure them with a sweet, hot drink to calm their nerves (a flash of a mug will do if you have no water, tea bags or sugar to hand). If they appear confused and unable to move, kindly point out their barge pole and explain what it is used for.

If a canoe approaches, ask the operator to hang on to the nearest available tree or shrub to prevent them from being sucked towards your fat boat. Most canoeists will automatically assume this position once your are within their sights, so continue with caution if this occurs.

Safety at locks

For the safety of other craft, it is wise to remind them that they will be unable to fit in the locks with you. Hire boaters will assume it is possible to fit in a gap of one inch, so stay calm and explain the situation to them. It takes on average 32.6 seconds for them to realise, so be patient. If in doubt, offer to go in first and ask them politely to follow.

Avoiding Suffocation

Remember to always leave your air vents clear on the boat. Although it is tempting to arrange slices of toast in them, or poke other amusing items into them, they're there for a reason, especially if you have a four-legged companion. Spending a night on a boat with a greasy, gas-filled dog is not a pleasant experience, and blocking the air vents can cause a serious incident, most usually resulting in the death of the dog.

Preventing babbling

To prevent towpath babbling about the width of your boat, there are several steps you can take to reduce the risk of anticipated comments.

Try painting your boat a dark colour, such as black. Avoid bright colours like reds that make the boat look even bigger and aggravate the public's reaction.

Failing a colour change, try painting or adding something unusual to your boat to spark comments about that item rather than the width. Tropical plants are a must, but tomatoes and marrows work equally well. Use them carefully. Illegal plants intended for other forms of consumption are _not_ recommended.

Paint the width of the boat in large letters on the side. This will prevent any confrontational arguments about just how wide your boat is. You might also like to paint 'Don't ask questions' on the side, as well.

If you get asked for a photograph, pose if it safe to do so, with arms as wide as possible. Foreigners in particular are very keen for photos of owners with their fat boats, and should not be discouraged from taking them at all costs. It is better to be appreciated than snubbed at for being fat. (The boat, not you).

*For entertainment only. This book and I are not responsible for your actions. It would be wise to not follow what I say and stick to the rules of the CRT handbook like glue for your own safety. That's why my rules never made the cut.

If you want to try the knots, feel free. Don't blame me if your boat blows away though, or if it takes several hours to untie. Remember, you're the one that tied it, not me.

Towpath Talk Special
February 2015
Internal Fascination

Over the past month our girl's interior has been coming on in leaps and bounds (except for the heavy kitchen cabinets which came on board with a little more care).

Engineer Dave and Dad struggled to push a monstrous beast of a cabinet onto her one morning and our girl responded by teasing them and drifting out as they stepped onto her, leading to some entertaining facial expressions and yoga positions, one of which we now call the 'splitting swan'.

The 'swearing duck' is a similar move, involving a swift flick of the head to hit the ceiling beam in just the right place.

My brother perfected the 'dipstick' move whilst he helped lift on the new stove, his trousers completing the look with a fetching tide mark for the remainder of the day.

We are now quite confident there is enough water in the canal but we may have to invite him back before the summer cracks on, just to double-check.

I'll make sure to send Canal and River Trust his number so that they can have him on speed dial to check against evapotranspiration issues.

Toilet seat chic

Meanwhile, Mum has been quietly beavering away with the soft furnishings and, as if by magic, an armful of cushions have appeared on the sofa, in the same fashion as mushrooms crop up overnight.

To protect them from harm, they've been nestled in their plastic packaging for weeks, the sofa to the point of becoming wrapped in a layer of cling film. We've all heard of the toilet seat trick before, and this achieves the same function; to embarrass you enough that you don't want to sit on it for fear of generating a farting noise in company.

Sign Writer Rob came aboard to say hello one grim afternoon, and froze in front of the sofa. He grabbed a cushion and cuddled it thoughtfully, momentarily saving it from his piercing stare.

'You are going to take the plastic off, aren't you?'

He pointed a shaking finger at the crime scene before him, horrified.

It's a good job there wasn't a chalk outline on the floor as well, or people might start to get the wrong impression.

The bathroom, too, is on its way to getting a makeover with its sparkling new white loo seat (the first one we bought didn't fit and the second one shattered in the post, hence we're saving them for a trophy wall. I can now understand why the courier threw it around in the van. No-one likes a toilet seat that takes forever to fit. Being soft close, it takes forever to shut as well).

I did plead for a silver glitter one I spotted in a department store, but judging by the looks I received from members of staff (and Mum and Dad) as I squealed in delight, I realised it might not be a good idea.

With only one toilet on board, you cannot afford to distract anyone's attention in there for too long. Reading material is also banned for the same reason, and there's now a stopwatch on the outside of the door, with 30.3 seconds maximum allowed for ablutions. Beyond that, you'll have to put up with the door being wrenched open and someone else diving in to brush their teeth – pants or no pants.

Thankfully, I don't ration toilet paper like someone else I know – you'll have a job using half a roll in the time limit, let alone three sheets.

Can cook, won't cook

The new kitchen on our girl proves to be an endless source of fascination to people, who instantly look for an oven.

Why they do this is a mystery. Personally, I only think about food 23% of the day, and yet, most of the people I know seem to think about it all the time. 'Where's your oven? How are you going to feed yourselves? Don't you cook?'

The answers are usually: 'The oven is at the dump. We go to the pub. We have new-fangled technology called an induction hob on which we can only cook half a breakfast at a time in a saucepan smaller than a teacup. We do have some tinned tuna, if you're hungry?'

You always get the wrinkles-above-the-nose look at this point, followed by a fast exit.

Our boaty neighbours on the far left (or right, depending which way round you stand) have the right idea. They have takeaways from a popular burger chain. If only there were 'drive-throughs' for boats. Now there's an idea.

5th January, 2015
Last Christmas I gave you my... toilet seat

Christmas wouldn't be Christmas without inviting a few (well-chosen) friends around for some nibbles and a nice warm by the fire. The one we've never lit properly before. The one we hadn't burnt off the paint fumes from. Hence, our first attempt was thwarted by the unintentional testing of the new smoke alarms.

After facing the complicated decision of which alarm to press the stop button of (there's 55ft between them), the doors, windows and swan hatch were thrown open so we could enjoy the fresh, minus one degrees marina air. Even Bolt would struggle running that many feet with a foggy mist and a passageway designed only for those with the most perfect sense of balance without falling sideways into the toilet as the other occupants of the boat dash in panic across the living room floor.

After fanning the alarms all morning, we worked up a fierce appetite, and whilst waiting for our guests to arrive, we tackled Mum's latest board game of 'sandwich roulette'. The beef ones are best for this – some have horseradish, some don't. Spinning the platter around so the next person has no idea is the best part. Never mind coughing over the stove fumes.

Once our guests were on board, things started to hot up (extra body heat for spatial warming works a treat), and the conversation got more and more interesting after a few rounds of beef sandwich roulette.

Then came vocal charades when none of us could remember the name of a popular brand of rubber gloves. Instead, we now call them mongooses. Sign Writer Rob says the fluffy trim on them is perfect for polishing windows and the like. Mongooses are a little hard to come by in the UK, but I do have my eyes on a neighbour's cat that would do nicely for a polishing trial, especially as it seems to have a knack already of walking up the boat gunnels and glaring in the windows at us. If it could polish with its stare, people would have to resort to sunglasses to look at the paintwork.

The only downside to lighting our new stove is the amount of condensation. We had an avalanche of ice slip off the inside of the windows the other day, and whoever sat on the sofa below the air vent had to suffer being randomly dripped upon in awkward places.

Polar bears now live under the floorboards, and if you've ever wondered why there are no penguins on the canal, it's because the entire UK population live on our boat in the cupboards. Even our boaty neighbours complain our girl is way too cold, and dread the day they are invited over for a winter's party. They even light their own fires day and night in an attempt to warm her up and avoid the cold emanating (and possibly emigrating) from her steel sides.

Wearing arctic gear and going to the toilet on a boat is a whole other matter entirely. We have a rule that if someone has not left the loo within five minutes, a search party breaks down the toilet door to unfreeze the unfortunate person from the toilet seat with one of those lighter sticks you use in the kitchen for doing the top of creme brûlées. Very painful – especially if you have a fondness for a sugary crunch on your dessert.

Fortunately, on the second party, we finally twigged the stove and had it roaring away like an English summer, whilst we sat around with our guests all afternoon in t-shirts eating lemon and toffee muffins and playing roll roulette (this time with tuna, egg or coronation chicken sandwich fillings). It's easier with rolls as you have the advantage of being able to lift up the top lid and check first.

A bit like the previous toilet seat, which, the day after our party we took great delight in taking to the local recycling facility to dispose of with a great clatter into one of the steel bins. Unsure of what material it was (you can never be too careful when it comes to choosing the right bin at the dump, in case Captain Jobsworth comes out of the hut to tell you off), we asked one of the chaps on duty who clearly didn't want to be associated with the disposal process and stood at a barge pole's length away holding his arm out to point. 'Plastics, mate, that's where that goes.'

We daren't tell him there was a tiny bit of metal in it too. And a few other things that are best left to the imagination.

The old front door steps went next with a huge lob into the wood bin, carpet topping and all, to make way for the nice new ones Handy Andrew has made us (minus the camel humps, of course). The great thing with the new steps is that they creak unexpectedly, no matter your weight. If you're smallish and you step on them and hear a huge crack, you panic and wonder how on earth you managed to put on so many pounds. If you're a bit more, well, you know, at the other end of the spectrum it's even more of a worry.

For us, it means visitors are less likely to steal our cakes and sugar, with their fear that the steps may not withhold them getting back out into the wild again.

Lemon muffin, anyone?

Towpath Talk Special
March 2015
Southerly Breeze

Trapped wind, combined with the sniffles, is perhaps the most terrible set of crimes on this earth – particularly if it involves an engine. Our girl caught one of those so-called nasties and refused to start, the bow shuddering as she coughed and spluttered, rocking in her foundations. We watched in horror as the great beast of green below the decks (her private parts) thrashed from side to side. It made a curious sound, a kind of cross between a sneeze, a chirping bird and a squirrel with indigestion.

Engineer Dave came to the rescue, looking upon her with a furrowed brow and a quizzical look on his face, before coming to the conclusion that she had trapped wind between her injectors. To put it into perspective, it was as bad as having wind stuck below your rib cage after drinking a pint of apple juice. Very nasty.

Unfortunately boats don't have the natural capacity to produce a jolly good fart, hence the need for a set of spanners and a great deal of patience to bleed her out like a radiator. I actually felt sorry for her, being in such an embarrassing situation. We all know what it's like to be in company when your body decides to misbehave.

Clean Pants

After some unpleasant fumbling, our girl was soon back to fighting fit under Engineer Dave's capable hands, and resumed to her normal rumble after a couple of turns of the engine key. I patted her gently. At least we used kitchen roll to mop up her spills, unlike the boxes of sanitised rags we often have, with curious examples of human undergarments in their midst. Knickers might be amusing, but, often being made of nice cotton, they are handy for cleaning purposes (when they too are clean and belong to someone else, of course. Using your own is against all righteous laws, and isn't an attractive quality to have).

The Theory of Neighbours

Suddenly, out of the blue, we have found that we have a new set of neighbours. The boat next to our girl has been sold, and not long ago we spied smoke coming out of the chimney – the ultimate 'I'm here' signal on a cold winter's day. I've since learned the hard way that it is far better to freeze than light your fire if you have your favourite type of breakfast muffins on board, or someone might just invite themselves in and eat the lot in front you whilst you look on like a dog that's had its bone whipped out from under its feet. Yes, you know who you are. The toffee flavour was my favourite one.

Once the new smoke was sighted, it seemed everyone in the marina had come outside to a). see if a new pope had been elected or b). paint/polish/nip to the shop/see Colin/walk the dog just to see what all the commotion was emanating from a small van carrying enough furniture for a small two storey house. Men were rushing backwards and forwards with sack trucks and chairs, and even I stopped to wonder how it would all fit (the boat is a fat one like our girl, so anything's possible).

Observers of this event were so curious and yet slightly afraid to see what was going on that they shouted to each other across the water just to see if anyone wanted a cup of tea so that they could confer with their theories in secret. Nursing theories is a very dangerous art, requiring two rounds of tea, lots of whispering and an initiation ceremony (no-one knows whether it involves dunking or drinking). Boaters are champions at shouting, being able to rival the yodellers of the mountains. After all, mobile phones are almost useless, and string and cups, well – quite frankly, it's better to yell across the marina and shout 'eh?' in response to every question. For some reason mouthing 'tea?' always gets a yes. Swearing achieves nothing except frowns from your neighbours.

I've yet to meet the new owners, but they sound interesting. I spied a cage big enough for a lion in their rear cratch, with a teddy bear bigger than me in it. Perhaps the bear is dangerous, who knows. Either way, our girl is now snug as a bug with two stoves (one each side) keeping her cosily warm for half the cost. Let's just hope she doesn't learn how to fart.

1st February, 2015
The Great Barge Bake-off

Winter is still holding on with its cold grasp, and hence, our girl has been tucked away cosily in the marina, awaiting our weekly return to check her water pipes and flick on the heating to briefly warm her heart. Together we long for each other once more, holding out for the chance of a warm spring day to lounge on the deck boards next to her and feed the swans.

Today, however, I was cheered by something of a revolution that my sister and her family had bought for me for my birthday. Unwittingly, they had changed my life, and possibly everyone else in the marina (if they catch wind of it).

It involves a book, a microwave, a china mug, ten minutes and some sugar, flower, eggs and most likely (in my case) chocolate. CAKE IN A MUG.

I need not say any more. My lifelong ambition once squashed by work commitments, time, and stress, will soon be fulfilled. No longer will I have the terrible fear on board of someone stealing my shop-bought muffins and other treats when they mysteriously 'drop by'.

With a cake disguised in a mug, no-one else stands a chance with my hands wrapped firmly around it. Even better, if I give them the recipe, they'll leave in double-quick time to go and make one for themselves.

When all you have in your galley is an induction hob and a microwave, the art of cake making would once have been an impossible mission; I now salute the author of the book I received for such an ingenious invention, nearly worthy of a Nobel Peace award.

With 600W and an appetite you can take on anything (except maybe emptying the toilet tank, as, admit it, no one is ever really prepared for that. The sight of chocolate cake can make such sights an even worse ordeal).

I once stared miserably at the cup of soup my work colleague makes from a sachet of powder that, when boiled from an overactive kettle, smelled and tasted like death warmed up. Now I laugh, flashing my microwave and new cake circle powers (and a marvellous smile, if I say so myself).

If only one could perfect a roast dinner in a mug, the boating universe would change forever. After all, Wales thrives on a delicious and fabulous dish called Cawl that's cooked in one pan (or an oversized mug, if you want to try).

Somehow, my boaty neighbours seem to manage cooking a normal roast. How they do this is a total mystery to me (however, it might have a lot to do with a full-sized gas oven). Apparently, it involves lots of shelf swapping at timed intervals — I've also heard rumours of much laying-on-the-back foot shoving as well.

I'll have to be careful my cake mixture doesn't exceed 21 x 29.7cm for fear the microwave door won't shut, or I'll have a queue of disappointed neighbours outside the kitchen window who look like they've turned up at the wrong Blue Dragon advert.

Some things are better kept behind closed doors. Especially mug cakes and roasts.

Remember, sharing cake recipes is very dangerous. Only do it in extreme situations, i.e you want to get rid of a visitor for talking too much/farting in YOUR boat/eating YOUR food which you planned on eating yourself/hogging the fireplace. Do it wisely, or friends may end up resorting to bad behaviour just to get one line of ingredients from you. You have been warned.

15th February, 2015
Panning for Gold

The birds have begun to sing triumphantly from the treetops, signifying spring is well and truly on its way.

Still too grim and cold for a gentle trip out on our girl, we decided instead to go for a steady walk on the towpath and catch up with a few friends, one of whom was rinsing out his saucepan in the canal from his swan hatch.

I've heard Fairy Liquid goes a long way, but perhaps this was a stretch too far. Terry the Paint is an ambitious friend of ours, so the only logical explanation was that he was panning for gold in the muddy flow.

Panning for gold in the canal is a dangerous game, and often you can expect the unexpected. Whole swedes, dead sheep, undergarments, floating unmentionables and hats can cause obstructions in the fine mesh required to achieve a handful of gold flakes. Perhaps the nearest anyone has got to it is a handful of cornflakes, which, quite frankly, are pretty expensive and are well worth collecting.

Terry shrugged when we asked him what he was doing, and so we settled on the thought that it could well be a new form of interactive water feature.

A boater next to us chuckled whilst we basked in the glory of his brilliant sky-blue boat with yellow accents. I haven't seen blue sky for a week what with being stuck in an office – I was tempted to ask him if it was possible to get a chair and sit within a foot of the boat so that I could pretend it was summer for a couple of hours.

The gentleman on it told us that apparently that morning the canal was as dry as a chip (hence Terry was still enjoying the novelty of it with his saucepan in the background). When he got up in the morning to step off the boat he thought he was on a mudflat and hit his head against the canal wall (which normally is less than half a foot above water level).

Instantly, we blamed someone leaving the lock paddles open, and the chap shook his head earnestly, a big grin on his face.

Oh, no, it was something much more exciting than that.

An entire herd of bull calves had escaped from the farmer's field the previous day and rampaged up the towpath, squeezing under the bridge and scaring the dog walkers to death, who turned and ran in the opposite direction (who wouldn't)*. One of the bulls fell in the water, splashed about and collapsed a huge chunk of wall section, leaving a nice big drain hole as if it had pulled an enormous bath plug.

We all know what a novelty it is to live with one leg longer than the other on a boat. Especially when it comes to relieving oneself in the bathroom. Blu-tac in these situations is a glorious and normally undervalued creation.

It does, however, beg the question – what do you do when confronted with a herd of bulls on a narrow towpath, armed only with a windlass, a British Waterways key and a mug of tea?

I'd ask Terry for his saucepan.

*I heard a story from a tertiary source several days later that one lady casually running up the towpath was stopped by a 'rough-looking boater' (don't worry, we all look like that, it's normal), who told her:

'You might want to take yer' top off, love'.

Of course, wearing a red Lycra top, and, being a lady, she assumed the worst and phoned the police.

Apparently the policeman laughed down the phone, and told her there was a herd of young bulls approaching her, and wearing red perhaps isn't the best idea.

Bulls aren't vain, but a lady swinging her top in the air with nothing on is enough to get any male into a furious rage of some sort.

Now I understand why most women don't wear clothes these days.

Personally, I'd rather wear camouflage.

Towpath Talk Special
April 2015
Spring Clean

Springtime usually goes hand-in-hand with something traditionally called a 'spring clean'. With one of those momentous thoughts in mind (the ones that seem a good idea until you try them, that is), we decided to get the bathroom shipshape for the oncoming season. Armed with a bucket, rubber gloves and sponges, Dad and I set to work – one of us scrubbing the floor, the other balanced over the bath on one leg in a ridiculous attempt to reach the other end (fixed shower screens aren't all they're cracked up to be). The Royal Ballet will soon be in contact to steal the outstanding choreography for their next show to be performed in a theatre the size of a shoe box.

For a moment, both of us pondered over the bath plug hole after considering tipping a bucket of water in it. A plug was left casually on the side (a gift from our girl's previous owners), and, after a fight to see who could reach it first, we shoved it proudly into the hole. It popped out again and again like a meerkat on speed dial each time we wedged it in. Confused, we looked around to see if there was some kind of mistake, that, my goodness, what happens if we have the curious urge to take a bath?

Just for the sheer frustration of it, we threw the bucket of water in anyway, then stared, agog. Thanks to the mysteries of modern boating, the water refused to budge. Both of us peered over into the black round thing, which defied all possible logic of a conventional hole. I'll give CERN a call soon, just to see if we might have discovered that peculiarity called 'dark matter' that no one seems to know the answer to. Explain a plug hole that isn't actually a hole, with zero gravitational pull (until we found the switch around the corner and it became a snorting, sniggering beast that sucked everything away). Such novelties.

Our girl however, had a very different perspective on spring cleaning and naughtily released her shower valves. Instead of the usual trickle from the shower head, a great jet blast out upwards from the taps like those big posh fountains found outside stately homes, and gave Dad a jolly good soaking. On Four in a Bed they complain about showers not having their controls on the outside. Ours doesn't have any control whatsoever.

Feeling Flushed

Once we had hung up our rubber gloves for the morning, we stood outside for a while and nattered to our boaty friends, who licked their dry lips when we mentioned we were off to the pub. We let them drool whilst we wittered on about burgers, cider, a warm fire and toilets.

One of our friends paused at this point, an eyebrow raised.

'The pub has a toilet? One of those that you can flush like this–'

He raised an arm and did the motion.

'Not like this?'

He pointed a finger as if to push a button.

We nodded earnestly in united persuasion.

'Cor, and I bet they have quilted toilet paper too, not that 'ard stuff.'

One of the general rules of consumption on a boat is not to use the type of loo roll that you could double up as a duvet cover unless you want to spend up to a week neck-high in something unmentionable with a box of spanners on your lap.

That's why lots of boaters spend plenty of time in pubs. It's not the drink they're after, but rather, somewhere comfortable to place their behind (and I don't mean in the bar, either).

Long-term Memory

It's also rather nice to think about where you might be placing the rest of yourself for a good night of sleep, hence I've purchased myself a mattress after discovering the ones left by the previous owners were alright for a hobbit's sleepover, but rather, shall we say, a little too skinny for someone who does sideways rolls in their sleep (the ones where you get that horrible jumping feeling and end up spread-eagled on the floor). Thankfully now there's a wall either side.

This mattress is awesome with a topper in memory foam. It means that if anyone else happens to lay down or sleep in it, I shall know, owing to the perfect imprint left of them. Why crime scene investigators haven't used this technique yet, I'll never know.

Quilted

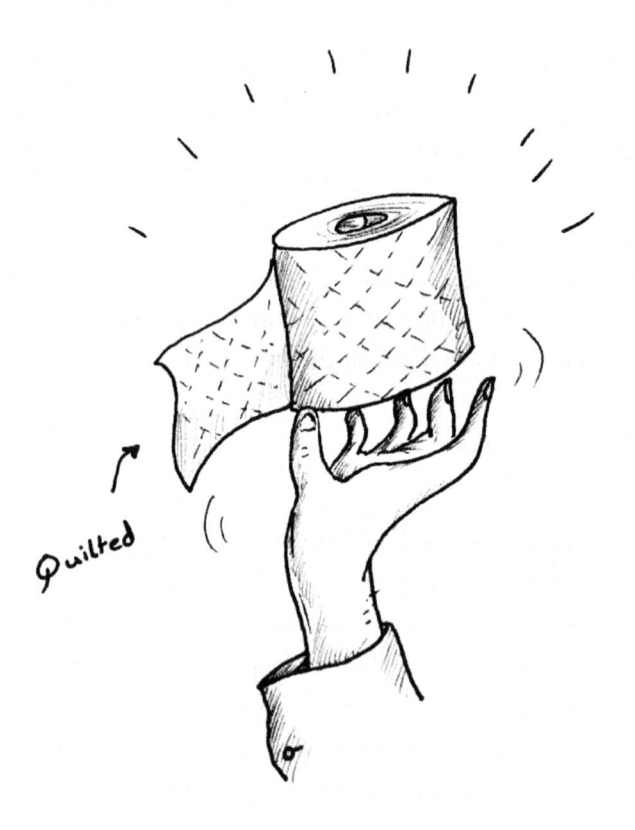

18th March, 2015
Giant Squid

Getting a mattress on a boat is a work of art in itself, but trying to get it through a 2ft corridor and around a 95 degree angle is a challenge, especially when the room it's going in resembles an elevator.

Mattresses aren't the most bendy-ist of things either. It was like trying to stuff an elephant into a wetsuit – the more I tugged, the more stuck it became, until, panting and puffing, I stood on top of the bed bent in half, arse touching the ceiling. With a grunt any tennis player would be proud of, the monstrous thing slid into place. I glared at it suspiciously and left it to its own devices whilst we prepared our girl with a few other items in anticipation of something called 'summer' and 'holidays', two words I've never heard of in two sentences, let alone together in one.

Mum's been slowly buying cushions over the past few months, in batches so that hopefully Dad and I don't notice the sudden invasion of puffed squares that continue to multiply like rabbits on the sofa. Eventually the living room will be so full of cushions it will be like a kiddies soft ball pool. Every time I straighten them I make sure they're an inch apart in case they have any ideas about hanky panky. I have the same problem with peas and mashed potato. Mixing them is against all laws of physics. And psychology.

We now also have a nice plastic box to keep our toothbrushes in (no flies on mine, thank you) and a bath mat in what is described as 'petrol blue'. Quite frankly, I've ever see blue petrol, and if it was that colour, everyone would want a transparent petrol tank, just for the fun of it.

Although planning ahead was entertaining, the weather itself was rather grim and uninviting, and we dared only stay for a short while before a trip to the pub for a well-deserved pint and a chat to some fellow boaters who were huddled out of the cold Easterly wind around the bar. Apparently it was the wind itself that had blown everyone in that day.

We quickly made some new friends who live permanently on their narrowboat, and have the most intriguing canal names of 'Badger' and 'Mouse'. I thought the names rather charming and endearing and far easier to identify than the usual 'Dave'.

Boaters are always so vibrant and exciting – they even cut their own hair. I admire them. I tried to cut someone's fringe once and it ended up something a Vulcan would be hugely disappointed with. Not a good look (hence why I don't have a fringe). It's just not logical.

I did overhear a snippet of conversation in the pub that consisted of 'giant squid' and 'canal'. Overhearing things is not good for you, and I went away terrified of the thought of those age-old books containing pictures of sea ships with masses of tentacles wrapped around them. I dread to think what lives in the Brassknocker Basin, what with it being over 12ft deep. If you see a fat boat speeding around the Dundas corner, you'll know why. I'm not hanging around to find out.

The next day we went in the pub again (the wind blew us in) and it was Mothers Day. Within seconds we were swamped by a group of men who looked as if they'd been exploring the arctic and needed a roast to defrost. Once they'd thawed and had a few pints, the conversation really got going. These chaps were holiday boaters who fiercely believed fishing was 'really only a form of maggot drowning', and 'what on earth is the point of sitting on the bank all day if all fishermen do is swear at boaters'.

People say that boating is a contact sport. Although bumping into boats all day is fun and amusing, 'contact' doesn't really exist between boaters and fishermen. They don't exactly swap numbers, either, preferring to ignore each other or, to another extreme, exchange rude words. Some boaters I've known have pulled a fast one and taken maggot drowning to a whole new level, rather drowning an entire box of maggots with a ginormous bow wave. How courteous.

These chaps however, didn't mind either way and soon finished their drinks and were off to be back in the wild again, joking that being down at the bottom of the locks meant it was all downhill, and far easier to walk back to their boat. They teased the smallest in their group, saying he could roll home what with whatever it was stuck to his front.

Personally, after a roast dinner and a pudding, I think anyone could have rolled home. My job was a bit harder, considering I live on top of a hill. The centre of gravity is all wrong up there. Hence I often stay a bit longer for another pint whilst my body assimilates dinner, alleviating the front load and swapping it to the back.

We're all longing for some warm summer sun and those long days once more, when there are more hours in the day for boating and giving holiday boaters some well-needed tuition. We love them, really. Just watch them move when I give them an award-winning smile and a fat boat on the end of a tiller.

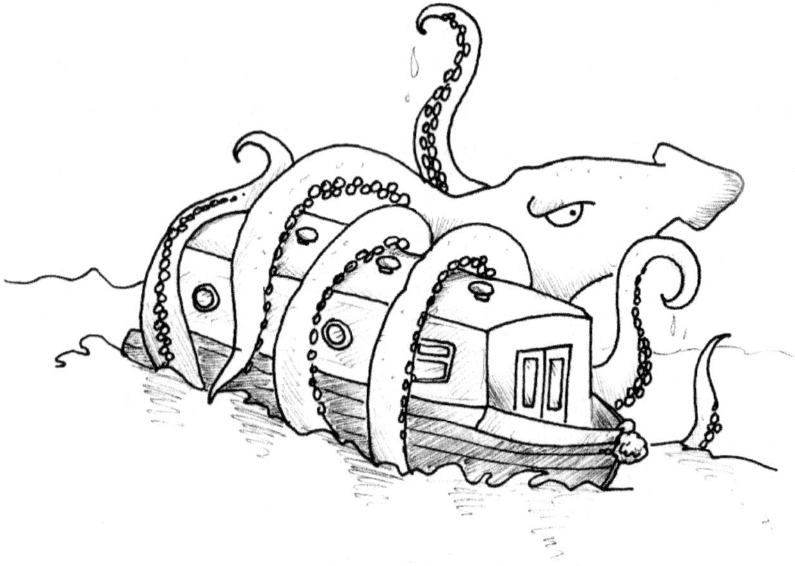

25th March, 2015
Silver Bullets

After finally putting down the paintbrushes, sponges, hand drills and rubber gloves, today was the epic day when we could say we had *finished* the interior of our portly girl. Except for one task.
The dreaded poo tank.

Sadly, the little gauge I fell in love with above the toilet doesn't actually move and has been stuck on zero for months. Evaporation is just not possible, and judging by the clean condition of the suitcases we found under the bed, there's definitely not a leak. (Mind you, a boater told me an interesting story recently how sweet corn isn't digested by the human body and comes out whole the other end, so a leek or two of the other kind could be possible).
We decided not to risk any dramas out on the cut this summer, so an empty was in order.

After weaving around the other moored boats and odd tufts of grass called islands peppered with ducks and geese, we made it to the service quay and the marina manager came over with a bucket and a big smile to help us. I didn't want to ask what the bucket was for, but decided it best to enjoy the picturesque Turner-like clouds whilst the pipe was inserted into our girl's bowels. The machine on the quayside shuddered and shook violently, as if it were sucking out demons from the tank. I had a terrible urge to fetch some garlic, a cross and some silver bullets, just in case something emerged, a bit like that film where a chap comes out of a vase in someone's living room. Instead, the marina manager pointed at the see-through tube. 'I can see what you've been eating!'

I dreaded to think. Last week was really topsy-turvey, what with a midweek roast, a pizza, fish cakes and a chilli con carne (not all on the same day, of course), followed by half a tonne of dried fruit and yoghurt. How he could tell all that was a mystery to me, and I dared not look, in case it revealed something about my personality. Raisins are enough to liven anyone up, especially if people are sat next to you. It does them more good than you.

After one final slurp, the machine was done. The monster left in the pipe gurgled one last goodbye, condemned for another year to live inside the steel case. So powerful and fast was this piece of kit, that our girl was practically sucked inside out. People on the Kleenex advert would say it's like wearing gold pants. There's nothing more satisfying than sitting on the loo with a nice empty tank at your disposal – I pledge to spray paint the loo seat gold, just so we get that everlasting golden glow applied to our cheeks.

Now the waste gauge no longer works, Dad has taught me a novel trick for determining how full the tank is by lifting the bed and tapping hard on the tank wall. I don't like to tap too hard in case the tank disintegrates and we end up with fossilised chunks distributed around the bedroom. I'm one of those 'soft' knockers who hate knocking a neighbour's door too hard in case it sounds angry/desperate/annoyed, or in some cases, in case my hand goes right through. At least boat doors are generally made of steel. We've trained a local woodpecker to sit on ours and drum every time someone squeezes it. It costs a fortune to keep what with all the neurofen and peanuts it consumes.

Thankfully the beds are now in place and the duvet sets are on, still wrapped in their plastic. There's nothing quite like fresh duvets still in their wrappers (even if they make crinkly noises when you sit on them). One of our bed sets has a giant map of the underground on it, just in case we take a wrong turn on the cut when on holiday and end up somewhere we shouldn't. The map is jolly useful for train buffs too.

And the plastic, in case you were wondering, is to stop the occasional drip entering the boat and spoiling the furniture.

Towpath Talk Special
May 2015
There and Back Again

Over eight long months of doing up our girl gave way to a recent and long-anticipated maiden 'sleepover' voyage, to be left free and to our own devices on the canal. Terrified of forgetting something, packing began over a week prior to the great event with everything from new pants down to fresh meringues (don't ask) smuggled on board.

As a present, I treated our girl to a traditional bugle horn – bored of our electric one and fed up with the sports canister one exploding my eardrums, I spent an afternoon practising blowing this one at home. Unfortunately, instead of producing a 'watch out big container ship approaching' sound I had desired, each time I blow it on cue all that seems to be produced is an amplified wet fart. At least everyone now knows it's us coming around the corner.

The trouble with having a sleepover (or holiday as it's more commonly known) is that generally, everyone has the same idea at the same time, and hence mooring for lunch becomes very much like the Germans with their beach towels (bless them). On the canal, dirty laundry makes for an excellent substitute, or failing that, simply standing a member of your crew on the bank with a windlass works a treat (don't lay them down as a. they won't like lying in a puddle and b. someone might get the wrong idea).

Just for Laughs

Once mooring up has taken place, an entirely new scenario unfolds in the form of holiday makers rushing by with their outstanding ability to hit both sides of the canal at the same time. It would be a terrible thought if they could manage to do the same with a car on the motorway.

Their antics, however, do make for an interesting afternoon's viewing on the bow with a newspaper in hand and, preferably, a plastic glass filled with wine (held very tightly).

We had one such afternoon whilst moored opposite the pub. A hireboat thundered by, tried to turn and thought it would be amusing to bump into a boat called *Giggles*, just for the laugh, and at the same time wedging themselves across the canal. Quite frankly, we had more to laugh about than they did, what with everything on board laboriously anchored with blu-tac (one should always be prepared).

Mum became bored of their disturbances that afternoon and decided to turn up the heat a bit by repeatedly turning up the television to full blast while watching an episode of NCIS. Hireboaters passed with terrified faces and revving engines when a blast of gunfire caught them unawares.

The following day we caught a holiday boat off-guard once more as we ascended a lock. Spotting us, one of them shouted: 'we're not going to get in a lock with $THAT$' (our girl was insulted) and they attempted a quick getaway to try to beat us to the next lock. But the mud had them, and we sailed by smiling and waving. (We did *try* to help them).

Fresh Fish

Lunch on holiday is also a pleasant experience, most of it of course, spent in the pub. As always, pub lunches are generally ENORMOUS and mine and Dad's eyes almost popped out of our heads when Mum's fish and chips arrived at the table in the shape of a battered whale. The table sagged under its sheer weight. The closest I have ever come to a sea creature of that enormity was a stuffed whale at Tring museum, and I dread to think if there were things like that swimming in the canal.

At the very least, most of the fish on the canal are now jolly respectable owing to the amount of toothpaste that goes out on to the cut each day (my dentist tells me to brush twice a day). Those said fish now have squeaky clean teeth and fresh breath owing to his advice. There's nothing worse than fishy breath.

Mum has other ideas about our next lunch when we stay on our girl again. Our fridge is always well-stocked thanks to her generosity, and she eyed up some tomatoes one afternoon after watching a cooking programme on television. Raymond Blanc suggested that tomatoes in a salad taste much better if they are sliced and 'macerated'. Seeing as we already have a macerator toilet, Mum presumed this means she can now flush the tomatoes down it a few times. I'm skipping the salad next time – it's all Raymond's fault.

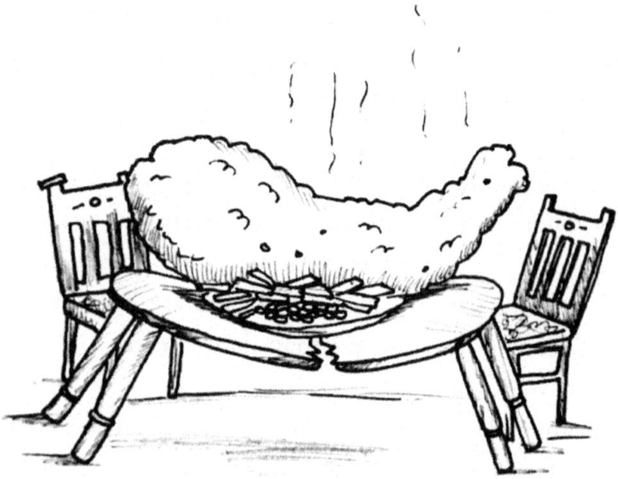

And Finally...

You're probably thinking – is that it? Is that all you've done? Why's the book so thin?

A) Although our girl's interior is now looking trim, there's a great deal to do externally. As every girl knows, having a fabulous exterior is pretty important.

> Sign Writer Rob is insistent she should be painted Ferrari Red.
>
> There's just one word for this: NO.
>
> We're going for purple, just to be weird.

B) Our girl will soon be having an inspection of her arse. I've given the canal-life stuck underneath a six-month eviction notice to prepare for this event.

C) The adventure doesn't end here. Our girl had a bath the other day with our super-duper new pressure hose, which ended up getting the sunbathing neighbours four boats down wet as well. Running from them is an adventure in itself.

D) I've deliberately made this book thin so you have room to store it between the loo rolls and the soap dish (try it for size) on your boat. We all know how difficult it is to fit the Lord of The Rings trilogy on board, for example.

Just, please, use this book wisely. And be nice to fishermen.

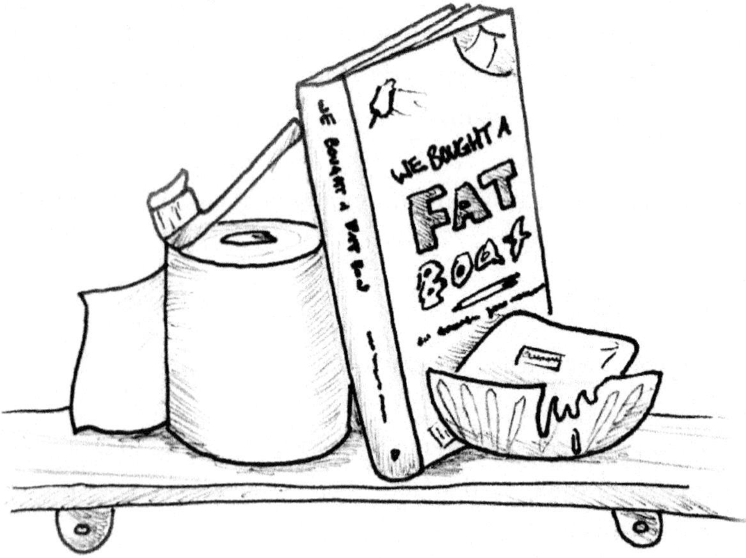
WE BOUGHT A
FAT
BOAT

The International Boater's Sign Language Guide

The following consists of a few helpful hints for those rather difficult boating situations where oral language is useless.

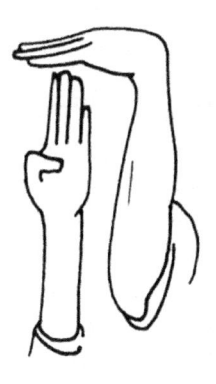

The Tea Break
Great for using to announce the kettle has boiled. Be wary of using it mid-argument or one may assume you're calling for time-out which could make the person intended for the message more frustrated.

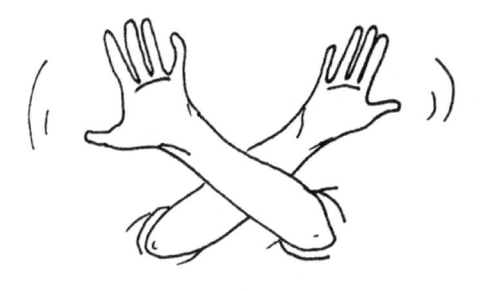

The Panic
Perfect for those dire moments such as 'don't do it', 'no!' 'stop!' Hire boaters have been known to confuse this with 'get out of the way' and often end up stranded in bushes etc.

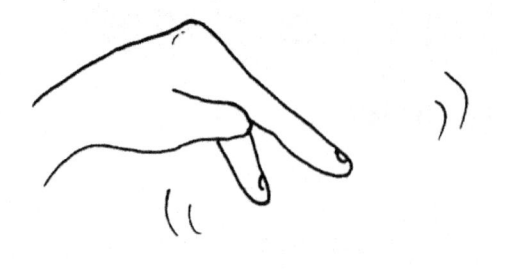

The Legless
The 'I'm walking to the next bridge/lock/etc'. Don't use this upright or people may assume you have a fetish for finger puppetry and laugh at you.

The Jaw-Jaw
Available for men or women to use, this one is normally directed to someone else with an accompanied roll of the eyes to suggest someone who talks too much. There are some fancy variations, but be careful not to be caught.

The Earache
A point of the ear suggests 'I can't hear you'. Be warned not to point at your temple instead, or the person may assume you're calling them a nutcase.

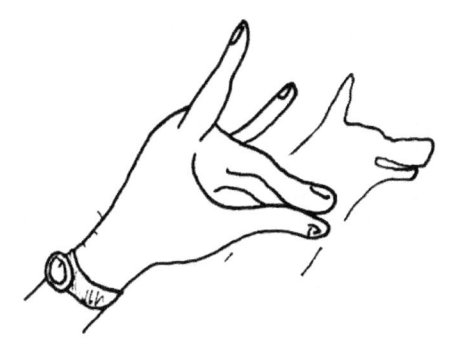

The Naughty Dog

Usually used when bored or trying to make kids laugh in the dark, this one can be varied by pointing the 'ears' down to suggest a dog having a poo on the towpath.

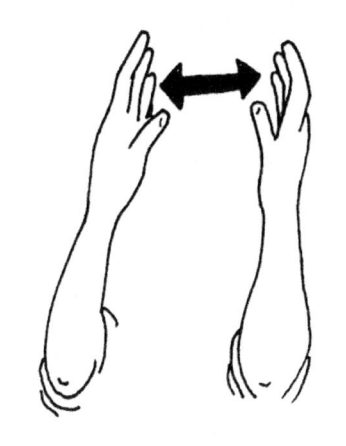

The Squeeze

Useful for directing the skipper on how close they are to objects. ALWAYS over-exaggerate. It makes for an interesting game. Their face normally resorts to a frown of utter confusion and an 'are you sure?' expression.

The Double Scout's Honour

Works as a greeting for those who follow a particular sci-fi series. Always handy for greeting hire boaters (no-one knows who they are anyway) and the Queen if you happen to see her.

CPSIA information can be obtained at www.ICGtesting.com
Printed in the USA
LVOW04s2007240815

451322LV00026B/865/P